MW00898785

SAT
ACT
TOEFL

College Prep
English Practice

SAT

ACT

TOEFL

College Prep
English Practice

English vocabulary, usage, comprehension,
and composition preparation for college and
college placement exams

K. Titchenell

ABACUS EDUCATIONAL SERVICES

EXCELLENCE IN EDUCATION
LIBRARY

Published by Abacus Educational Services, Altadena, California

ISBN-13: 978-1461083801

ISBN-10: 146108380X

Printed in the United States of America

First Edition

http://abacus-es.com/cpep

Who Should Read This Book?

This book is intended for English speakers or advanced ESL speakers who want to augment their vocabulary and improve their language and writing skills in preparation for college, college entrance exams or for writing and publishing in English.

Table of Contents

Introduction

This is not a preparation manual for any specific test, though it covers the content of most English proficiency tests quite thoroughly. The SAT, ACT, TOEFL and other exams purport to assess competence in English language usage to determine whether an individual will succeed in an environment where that proficiency is required. Whether it is possible through tricks and stratagems to score well on an exam in the absence of that proficiency is a matter of dispute, but there is no question that English proficiency is of greater and more lasting value than the skills involved in exploiting the flaws and predictable patterns of a specific exam. Mastery of the English language is one of the world's most valuable accomplishments and the ability to demonstrate that language competence in interviews, applications, essays and published works often carries more weight in the college entrance process than does an examination score.

These pages are intended to provide the student striving to handle college-level English with an enjoyable romp through the acquisition of language proficiency and the skill to determine and comply with current language usage standards readily and comfortably. The high school junior or senior, the advanced ESL student seeking to study in English at university, or the foreign academic seeking to publish in English would all find this work to be of value.

The ability to express thoughts clearly, coherently, and persuasively is an essential skill in college, in the workplace and indeed anywhere in the modern world. Even those whose role in society requires little or no communications skills will benefit occasionally from the ability to describe an event and write a convincing letter or, failing that, will suffer from the inability to do so at the hands of those who can.

What is Correct English?

What does it mean to speak and write correctly? What standard, what set of rules, whose example should the student aspire to? There actually exists an irrefutable answer to these questions.

Very simply, correct language usage is that which conveys to the intended audience the message and the impression the writer or speaker would like to give. Really this is the only measure that counts. Let's call it the **Reader Rule**. To the extent that the reader receives the intended message and impression, the language is the correct choice. It then only remains to determine what that language is, given a specific body of readers.

If the readers or listeners are college professors or academic colleagues, the appropriate written language is probably a fairly formal variety of Standard English (SE), depending of course on the relationships involved. In other environments – the construction site, jazz studio, football pitch, gridiron, rodeo circuit, oil rig, prison, in various corners of the military – the language treated here might be largely inappropriate and ill suited to acceptance and camaraderie. The languages that would be fitting in these environments, while beyond the scope of this book, can certainly be researched, scrutinized and emulated using the methods here presented – to the extent that they are accessible in some recorded form on the Net.

In the academic or literary worlds and in most realms of business, one would rarely ever be censured for not breaking a grammar rule, for not misusing a word according to its dictionary definition or for not failing to tie the parts of a sentence together properly. On the other hand, committing such errors may well be a cause of embarrassment and opprobrium. In most cases, well-crafted academic language differs very little from one English speaking country to another and when it does, the minor spelling and stylistic variations would only very rarely impede complete comprehension. It is for those who would communicate and interact comfortably in these realms that this book was written.

A Comprehensive Treatment of Current Language Usage

No work can realistically aspire either to cover such a massive subject as the English language exhaustively or to remain current with its ever evolving diction. It is possible however, given access to the Internet, to examine examples, to determine which of multiple alternatives is most commonly used, and to do so more rapidly and accurately than would be possible in an ever-current hardcopy book of infinite size were one to exist. This scrutiny of Web literature for quantitative language analysis can also be specifically targeted by limiting one's search to only university websites, those within a specific university, academic sites within a specific country, only literary sites, or special interest corners of the Internet which may well include non-standard dialects used in specific regions or professions. The skill to use search engines for this purpose, as described and practiced in these pages is easily acquired and, when second nature, can immensely improve the conformity and confidence of one's prose.

It must be noted however, that good, creative, expressive writing does not necessarily conform to norms. In some ways, such conformity can be an inverse measure of a work's literary value. If one were to try to find an online copy of a particular newspaper article by searching for the occurrence of a specific quote, one might well discover that the vapid and unoriginal style used by many journalists renders this difficult or impossible, as every phrase in their writing seems to be drawn from a common pool of insipidity. On the other hand, the expressive screeds of highly regarded award-winning journalists such as Robert Fisk or Christopher Hitchens often contain so many unique verbal juxtapositions that even a short article can contain dozens of excerpts found nowhere else on the Web. (Note that "common pool of insipidity" is, at least at the time of writing, an example of one such unique phrase.)

As with any art, the student must understand and appreciate prevailing standards and then eventually learn to wield creative devices in ways demonstrating inspiration and individuality. This work covers strategies for readily determining and following predominant English usage but also pushes boundaries somewhat, providing examples and inspiration for exploring creative originality.

Some material here presented appeared previously in *SAT Practice: The New Verbal Section,* Abacus Educational Services 2004, but has been augmented and updated for the present volume. These chapters were written as weekly exercises for an Advanced Writing and College Preparatory English course and an ESL class for homeschooling students at *Excellence in Education*, the definitive homeschool resource center in Monrovia California. Material presented to students attending voluntarily, particularly those who have never been conditioned to accept unquestioningly a curriculum imposed upon them, must hold the interest and must convey useful material while the interest is there. These chapters accomplish that by providing engaging lessons densely packed with content.

The reading selections, reading comprehension quizzes, and suggested composition topics are designed to cover language material which will be of lasting value to anyone preparing for college and college entrance, and to do so in a way that is accessible to students of varying ages with a wide range of learning styles. In classroom testing, both in College Preparatory English and ESL classes, they have effectively held the attention long enough to convey their highly concentrated instruction very successfully.
Students preparing for college entrance are told that the single most effective thing they can do in preparation for college entrance exams is to read extensively and thereby build their vocabulary and become conversant with great writing and language

used well. While this may be true in the larger scheme of things, one would need to read vast quantities of literature to see a significant proportion of the challenging vocabulary and literary devices found in this volume with its accelerated approach. By presenting words in meaningful context with side-by-side definitions and sound recordings, then adding glossaries with synonyms and word variants, reading comprehension quizzes, usage notes and worksheets, and suggested writing projects, a great deal of ground is covered in a very short time.

The emphasis placed upon "reading" as such should also be brought into question. Until recently, the book was indeed the only medium for accessing the knowledge of the world but, as audio and video versions of almost everything are now universally available, this is no longer the case. Many students will find that an auditory approach suits their learning styles better, and for this reason, the reading passages are available in audio form as well as hardcopy. Appendices include a comprehensive glossary, parts of speech reference, verb conjugation algorithms, verb phrase construction rules, a table of Greek and Latin roots, prefixes, and suffixes, and a collection of online resources.

Whether language texts should prescribe ideal usage or describe prevailing usage has been long debated. The examples in this volume were created using both traditional reference works and quantitative analysis of English as it is used on the web as a whole and in selected academic sites. However, when words are considered that have found their way into common parlance due to ignorance of a more appropriate word, often through the fumbling inarticulacy of public figures, popular practice may be superseded by the more scholarly alternative. As we will see when sampling English usage, findings based on the Web as a whole may well contradict those drawn specifically from academic sources.

The juxtaposition of frivolity and erudition used in these reading passages and usage examples may no doubt seem incongruous and even ludicrous to some, but it seems to work well for its intended audience. It has been convincingly demonstrated that seeing and using a word in context will help one learn the word. It is also true that the dictionary definition of a word frequently falls short of presenting enough information to use that word in context with confidence. The present work provides context in bite-sized portions of largely original material written specifically around the vocabulary itself. Brief enough to be easily memorized, the reading selections can be spread out, one a day, and still be completed in a reasonable period of time, or they may be consumed in a single gulp. The reader will also be prepared to explore with ease and confidence the demotic usage of words and expressive devices as implemented by English language experts and the English speaking world as a whole.

To those who find omissions, oversights, or mistakes, our profound apologies. To those unable to appreciate frivolity and general silliness, our deepest sympathy.

Acknowledgements

Much thanks is due to Martin and Caroline Forte of *Excellence in Education* for their support in the project and Caroline Forte for her editing contributions. Appreciation is also due to Shakespeare, Monty Python, A. A. Milne, P.G. Wodehouse, Kenneth Grahame, Douglas Adams, Oscar Wilde, Edward Lear, Dr. Seuss, Bruce Hall, Stephen Fry, the Brothers Grimm, and many others for their words, whimsy, inspiration, and/or lunacy.

Conventions Used

Each chapter contains a reading selection with a side-by-side glossary; an extensive glossary with definition, synonyms, and word variants; a reading comprehension quiz; English usage notes; and suggested writing projects.

Standard American typography dictates that when a phrase or sentence ends with quote, the terminal punctuation should appear inside the quotes. In order to be perfectly clear about what belongs in the quotes and what does not, this convention has not been used here. Instead, the practice of including in the quote only that which belongs in the quote has been adopted. This is common in Britain and it is hoped that the reader will not be confused or offended by this policy.

As this work is intended for those who actually want to learn and not necessarily for a classroom in which students are to be kept frustratedly guessing and in the dark about their mistakes pending

grading and official revelation, quizzes and playsheets are followed immediately by the answers rather than having their answers secreted at the end of the chapter or back of the book.

Only verbs, nouns, and adjectives are listed in the glossaries because these are the only parts of speech that most students need to
learn.   Adverbs are generally derived from adjectives and when
such an adverb is used, the glossary usually lists the correspond-
ing adjective instead.

A term may have multiple forms.   A verb may, for example, also
exist as a noun, an adjective, or perhaps all three parts of speech.
In these cases an effort has been made to give all commonly used
variants of the word.   Here are a few examples of words with all
three forms:

verb	adjective	noun
evade	evasive	evasion
abstain	abstemious	abstinence
hypothesize	hypothetical	hypothesis
adulate	adulatory	adulation
defame	defamatory	defamation
intuit	intuitive	intuition
jubilate	jubilant	jubilation

By using its progressive form, any verb may be converted into an
adjective that modifies the subject of the verb.

For example:
Verb: exasperate   adjective: exasperating
> *The exasperating bureaucrat ignored the growing queue of*
> *patient applicants.*

Those verbs which take an object (transitive verbs) may also use
their participial form to modify the object of the verb.

Verb: exasperate, adjective: exasperated
> *The exasperated applicant sang and juggled magazines until the bureaucrat could no longer ignore him.*

These adjectival verb forms should only be used when no preferred adjective exists. For example, one could say *the adulating language of the letter was fulsome and nauseous,* but it would be far better to say *the adulatory language of the letter was fulsome and nauseous* because the word *adulatory* is an established adjective. It is perfectly acceptable to use the progressive or participial verb forms as adjectives if nothing better exists. With a few exceptions, there was no need to cite these adjectival verbs among the word variants as their existence can be universally assumed.

Many adjectives can be made into nouns by simply adding the ending *ness*: fatuousness, confusedness, parsimoniousness. However, these are generally to be avoided in favor of other forms *fatuity, confusion, and parsimony,* when available. Most nouns formed using *ness* are omitted from the glossary.

Although, when learning vocabulary, one concentrates primarily upon verbs, nouns and adjectives, other parts of speech, pronouns, conjunctions, prepositions, etc., compose a major proportion of the language we use. These are relatively few in number however, and most English speakers already know them fairly well. They are covered at length under prepositions in Appendix B P240. Learning the role that prepositions play in coloring the meaning of verbs and nouns, however, presents a major hurdle for students.

Verbal Phrases and Collocation

A solid and reliable feel for idiomatic language is one of the most difficult skills to acquire and the correct choice of preposition to convey the intended meaning is critical. There are not very many prepositions to worry about. Here is a fairly complete list:

aboard, about, above, across, after, against, along, amid, among, anti, around, as, at, before, behind, below, beneath, beside, besides, between, beyond, by, despite, down, during, except, excepting, excluding, following, for, from, in, inside, into, like, near, of, off, on, onto, opposite, outside, over, past, per, plus, round, save, since, than, through, to, toward, towards, under, underneath, unlike, until, up, upon, versus, via, with, within, without.

As we learn verbs and nouns however, we must also note which prepositions are used with them and how they affect the meaning of the word. Let us examine, for example, the verb "take" and consider the differences in meaning conveyed by:

take on	*undertake or confront*
take off	*to remove an article of clothing or the launching of an aircraft*
take over	*to capture, overrun*
take out	*to go on a date (with someone)*
take in	*to provide accommodation (for someone), to observe*
take after	*to emulate or resemble (someone)*
take back	*to retract*
take apart	*disassemble*
take down	*to record (in writing), to subdue (someone)*
take for	*to misidentify (someone as someone else)*

Some of the terms in these chapters must be used with the correct prepositions. Without knowing the correct preposition to use with a noun or verb, knowing its definition is of little use. For example, the noun *aversion* and its synonyms use a number of different prepositions: It is *aversion to* but *dislike of/for*, *loathing of*, *distaste for* and *hatred of*. When a term is associated predominantly with one or two specific prepositions, chapter glossaries will indicate those prepositions in square brackets ([]) with the more commonly used one given first based on web usage frequency. More importantly, the reader will learn to determine quickly and easily what the prevailing usage is by direct study of web usage.

Taking College Entrance Exams

The SAT and ACT are standardized tests used for admissions purposes by United States colleges, together with other factors including class rank, G.P.A. and extracurricular activities.

The TOEFL (Test of English as a Foreign Language) is often used as an admissions requirement for non-native English speakers at many English-speaking colleges and universities around the world. It is also used by government agencies, businesses and scholarship programs as a measure of English language proficiency. Unlike the SAT and ACT examinations, TOEFL scores are only valid for two years, as it is assumed that language proficiency will likely change in that period of time.

All of these exams purport to assess competence in English language usage to determine whether an individual will succeed in an environment where that proficiency is required.

The SAT

The SAT (formerly the Scholastic Aptitude Test) is published by the College Board (http://sat.collegeboard.com) which maintains that it is not possible to coach students successfully to take the exam and that specific test preparation has had a very minor effect on test scores. Test preparation books and services do of course present an opposing viewpoint, in some cases maintaining that test prep is more important than knowledge of the subject. The truth is clearly somewhere in between.

It makes absolutely no sense to waste precious test time reading instructions and learning the layout and timing of the exam. It clearly does make sense to know these things in advance and to look at real SAT questions to get a feel for what the test setters are looking for. The only way to accomplish these is to study the official College Board publication, *The Official SAT Study Guide* (current edition), because that work is copyright and is the only source for real SAT tests.   Practice the tests with the clock running to get a solid feel for the testing environment and your own abilities.

The stated purpose of the SAT is to provide an accurate measure of math and verbal skills.   Many test preparation books and services purport to defeat this stated purpose by presenting tricks and strategies with which a student with limited knowledge can do well on the test.   The College Board of course does everything it can to prevent this.

There certainly are some tricks that are worth knowing, but these are relatively simple for the most part.   As tests will eventually be published after they are retired, every correct answer must be irrefutably correct and every wrong answer absolutely wrong.   The answer is therefore always stated unequivocally in the question.

Critical Reading

These sections generally start with 5 to 8 sentence completion questions, with the following questions based upon reading passages.   In all sentence completion questions, the answer is clearly stated in the question, but the wording is different.   An understanding of the vocabulary and context is all that is needed to choose the right answer.

Questions based upon reading passages are generally ordered according to the flow of material in the passages but may have one or two out of order. The answers are nearly always clearly stated, albeit in different words, with only one or two that require inference.   In some cases a pair of quotes are presented and the student is required to conclude the intent of each author. Understanding that these answers are designed to stand up to a high level of scrutiny after the fact is very useful in determining the correct answer. The reading comprehension questions in the following chapters are designed exactly the same way the SAT questions are.

In the critical reading section, vocabulary and context sensitivity are key. Practice these multiple times with a timer.

The Writing Section, Multiple Choice Questions

The test-taker is asked in multiple choice questions to find the error in a sentence and to identify which of several variants of a sentence or paragraph is clearest and most idiomatic. Again, the correct answer must always be ineluctably correct and the wrong answers unquestionably wrong. To the student of grammar, usage and vocabulary, the correct answer is usually quite evident.

Unlike the reading section in which questions address the reading passage sequentially, in this and other sections the questions are more difficult at the end of a section than at the beginning. Many people find that the most obvious answer is usually the correct one at the beginning of a section, but often the wrong one toward the end of a section.

Points to watch for:
- Subject/verb agreement
- Avoidance of fragments and run-ons.
- Correct parallelism
- Elimination of redundancy
- Avoidance of awkwardness
- Economy of verbiage
- Correct punctuation and capitalization
- Clarity
- Correct use of collocation
- Tricky, unintuitive answers toward the end of each section.

These are all addressed on the following pages.

One particular grammatical error to watch for is synesis, as this is a grammar point upon which the SAT position differs from that of the rest of the English speaking world, including academia. (*See* Synesis Error p200.)

After covering the material in this volume, the student should be able to handle with reasonable certainty the questions presented in the writing section.

The Essay Section

Always the first section of the test, the essay section requires the student to produce a first draft of an essay in 25 minutes and in response to a specific prompt which is intended to require no prior knowledge. The essay is then read by two readers and then by a third if the grades allotted by the first two differ. The College Board states that examples used in essays should be drawn from the student's "reading, studies, experience, or observations".

It is important to understand that the essay grading process is the only part of the exam that requires attention and time on the part of the testing service, and that it will not get very much of either. It has been fairly well demonstrated that the grade allotted to a paper is, with greater than 90% accuracy, directly proportional to the number of words in the paper – the longer the paper, the better the grade.

In all probability, a good topic sentence clearly related to the prompt is a good place to start and it is, in all likelihood, best to make it the first sentence of the introductory paragraph to increase the odds that it is actually read. Some sophisticated structures and vocabulary may also be advisable – if you have to produce a quantity of prose anyway, you might as well have fun with it as long as it doesn't slow you down. As no fact checking is ever done, examples needn't be drawn from sources and may be invented on the fly, thus, to the creative mind, the possibilities are

endless. Take time to practice producing papers in 25 minutes.
This is a skill that can be improved and developed. The suggested
writing projects at the end of each chapter should help in practic-
ing this.

Points to remember:
- Write a lot.
- Use sophisticated language
- Use vocabulary
- Use paragraphs
- Don't' stop writing
- Make stuff up

It never hurts to have a couple of stock phrases handy, probably
for starting and ending the essay. If asked to present arguments
for or against a specific point for example:

> *While it has been irrefragably established that [the pro
> argument] the [con argument] also has merit and some
> staunch proponents which cannot be ignored.*

It's not wise to use this example of course. Take some time and
make something up ahead of time, a sentence into which any topic
can be inserted with a minimum of revision. Get a parent or
teacher to check it over.

Practicing for the SAT

Those for whom timed test taking is a new experience (often the
case with homeschoolers) sometimes find the time constraints to
be oppressive and any noises distracting. Some students have
found timed practice test taking with a loud ticking clock to be
very effective preparation.

The ACT

The questions on the ACT (http://www.act.org/, originally American College Testing) are thought to be somewhat easier than those on the SAT, but time constraints are greater. The ACT is more popular in the middle of the US, with the SAT predominating on both coasts.

English

The 45 minute first section consists of 75 questions on usage, mechanics and expression. Five passages are presented with options to improve their usage and mechanics including punctuation, misplaced and dangling modifiers, fragmentary and run-on sentences and the organization of paragraphs. The solutions are fairly easily determined by the student with a reasonably intuitive feel for writing style and an understanding of basic writing mechanics.

Reading

Four passages drawn from fiction, social science, humanities and the fine arts and the natural sciences are the subject of 40 reading comprehension questions to be answered in 35 minutes. Unlike SAT reading comprehension questions, a certain amount of deduction and inference is expected but, as is the case on the SAT, wrong answers are clearly wrong, generally asserting facts that are not present in the passage.

The TOEFL Internet Based Test

The TOEFL is composed of four sections to be completed in four hours. Emphasis is upon the language encountered in an academic environment. The test may be retaken but no more than once a week.

Reading

Reading selections on undergraduate-level academic subjects are presented with multiple choice questions to answer focusing upon causality, argumentation, comparison and general rhetoric. No prior knowledge of the subject is relevant to answering correctly.

Listening

The taking of notes during the section is permitted and highly recommended as the passages, conversations or lectures are heard only once. Five questions are asked about each conversation and 6 about each lecture. The ability to understand main ideas and details and to recognize the purpose and attitude of the speaker are evaluated.

Speaking

There are two different types of speaking sections, one in which in which test-takers respond to opinion questions on generally familiar subjects, and four sections in which the test-taker is expected to integrate material from both spoken and written input. Topics covered are campus life, lectures or conversations and test-takers are given a short preparation time and then their ability to conflate information from reading and listening material and express it effectively in speech is evaluated.

Writing

The writing section consists of two parts. In one, the test-taker reads a passage on an academic subject and then listens to a speaker discussing the same topic, then summarizes the important points in the listening passage, explaining how they relate to the written passage. In the other, test takers are asked to write an essay that takes a stance on an issue, supporting their positions and opinions with solid arguments.

Preparation: practice listening to and summarizing speech. Practice taking notes. Practice supporting an opinion with arguments in both speech and writing. Above all, listen to a lot of well-spoken English. There are many examples of speeches, interviews and debates available with language that ranges from poor to superb. See our listening resources section for examples of the latter at http://abacus-es.com/cpep

Perhaps most important, with this and all other reading, keep a vocabulary journal containing any new words encountered. Make a point of studying how they are used properly in context by searching them in academic sites (*See* Searching for Usage in Academic Sites p14) and practice using them correctly.

Chapter 1

Vocabulary: Boadicea Arrives on Stichwort Campus

Boadicea enjoyed a stimulating home-schooled environment and thus had some difficulty deciding upon a major in college, eventually, after much negotiation, undertaking interdisciplinary multiple majors in economics, fine arts and electrical engineering. She rapidly overcame the **stigma** of being a **dilettante**, while gaining a reputation as a **polymath** after her highly successful musical setting of her uncle Aloysius's **prenuptial** agreement which was performed **a cappella** at his wedding, receiving rave reviews and then becoming **syndicated** among wedding planners nationwide.

stigma n. disgrace
dilettante n. dabbler
polymath n. person of varied learning
prenuptial adj. before marriage
a cappella adj. unaccompanied
syndicated adj. widely published

This success was soon overshadowed by her invention of anti- stutter / anti **anosmia** programmable earplugs and then her remarkable art exhibition which included the award winning painting *The **Muses** Contemplating an Egg whisk.*

anosmia n. loss of sense of smell
muse n. god of inspiration

It was only after her founding of *The Society for **Conscientious Deferential Irreverence*** (SCDI) that she realized

conscientious adj. following the conscience
deference n. courteous respect
irreverence n. insolence

her full potential however. The SCDI inspired writers, sculptors, actors and other artists to use their skills to showcase and remedy ills of society, starting with the **stagnation**, **atrophy** and neglect for student needs that had become common in some colleges.

> stagnation n. lack of vitality
> atrophy n. deterioration through lack of use

Boadicea's Uncle Cuthbert who had assumed the office of Vice President of Institutional Direction and Credentialing (IDC) at Stichwort College the previous semester was therefore horrified to discover that she would be enrolling as a special-status student at Stichwort in fall.

His **protestations** and **remonstrations** had met with universal **pretermission** from Boadicea and the rest of the family as there were no justifiable grounds upon which to legitimate a **ban**, though nobody who knew her doubted that her presence would likely lead to **tumult** and **upheaval**. She had in fact come for the express purpose of founding a chapter of the SCDI, though her arrival had gone largely unnoticed elsewhere on campus. Uncle Cuthbert had no desire to **apprise** others in the Stichwort administration of either her **predilections** or their kinship and retained the fond hope that the latter might remain undiscovered.

> protestation n. dissent
> remonstration n. objection
> pretermission n. ignoring
>
> ban n. prohibition
>
> tumult n. commotion
> upheaval n. disruption
>
> apprise v. inform
>
> predilections n. tendencies

Boadicea was not at all surprised by the state of the college as it was fairly typical. Core subjects in many departments had become **egregiously superannuated**. Many professors had taught their **obsolescent** subjects with the same **vapid** language, references and identical homework assignments (in some cases oblivious to the repeated submission of the same paper on over a dozen occasions) every semester for several decades and expected retirement to precede any **ineluctable mandate** to modify their approach.

Classes of little interest and no **intrinsic** value abounded among offerings, kept alive by an intricate mesh of **reciprocal pre- and co-requisites**. Languages, history, philosophy and the arts had been **eviscerated** in favor of technology, business and the hard sciences. The administration and counselors had many policies and agendas in which benefit to the student and society played a rather minor role.

Textbooks were horrifically expensive and, despite annual new editions – **purportedly** issued to keep content current but in reality consisting only of cosmetic changes intended to hinder trade in used texts – remained several years behind current research and practice. Degrees and certificates continued to serve as **enticements** to students who would invest years in pursuit of the unattainable – required classes for

Egregious adj. conspicuously bad
superannuated adj. out-of-date
obsolescent adj. obsolete
vapid adj. uninteresting

ineluctable adj. unavoidable
mandate n. command

intrinsic adj. essential

reciprocal adj. mutual
prerequisite n. advanced requirement
eviscerate v. disembowel

purported adj. supposedly

enticement n. temptation

completion of their goals having been cancelled or rarely offered and then only by **senile**, **draconian** and **atavistic** professors.

senile adj. doddering
draconian adj. harsh
atavistic adj. throwback

The coffers of the college were typically depleted by its policy of silencing **detractors** (handling well-founded lawsuits by granting generous settlements contingent upon adherence to

detractor n. critic

strict confidentiality agreements) in preference to taking the necessary steps to amend or cease its **tortious** practices.

tort n. civil offense

Before the newly constituted chapter of the SCDI had met a second time in the tiny office allotted them in the back of the audio-visual building just behind that of the *Unrepentant Recovering Reductionists*, a massive statue had appeared in the main quad depicting an **emaciated** student **laden** with an impossibly **prodigious fardel** of **exorbitantly** expensive textbooks, their $100 - $200 price tags still prominently visible. Only after being struck by this sight did the viewer notice a smaller display composed of two figures clearly labeled "Textbook Publisher's Representative" and "Professor" at an **sumptuously** laden table with a pile of boxes displaying labels such as "Guaranteed No-Embarrassment Lecture Notes", "Effortless Power Points", "One-Click Essay Evaluation Software", "The Online Test and Gradesheet Creator" and a single small packet, not on the table, labeled "Barbados Educational Retreat".

unrepentant n. remorseless
reductionist n. one who breaks a problem into smaller parts
emaciated adj. thin
laden adj. burdened
prodigious adj. massive
fardel n. burden
exorbitant adj. excessive

sumptuous adj. lavish

Several educational blogs, a local paper and an online Gujarati newsletter specializing in educational protests ran illustrated stories on the statuary and the Provost was inundated with questions before she had even had an opportunity to see it. The dean who had signed the approval for the display was interrupted in the middle of a meeting with the **Kantian Culinary** Creationists and urgently summoned to Uncle Cuthbert's IDC office (which was being referred to with increasing frequency as the office of Idiocy Damage Control).

Kant proper noun a philosopher
culinary adj. related to cooking

Uncle Cuthbert's fears had been justified. After photos of textbook representatives were posted on the SCDI website, visits from those representatives became far less frequent. Several professors adopted inexpensive trade books for their classes and professors Trefusus of Western Philosophy and Finnek of the Classics department did not adopt texts at all, opting instead for customized collections of public domain web-based material.

Laudation by the SCDI which included the *Trevusian Oratorio* and the *Finnek Rap* quickly made these into celebrities and filled their classes to capacity – a rare occurrence both in Philosophy and Classics. Several students changed their majors and the Trefusus and Finnek Rate-My-Professor pages became flooded with **approbatory** postings.

laudation n. praise

approbatory adj. approving

Glossary

a cappella adj. adv. Sung without instrumental accompaniment.

anosmia n. The inability to smell or sense odors. Anosmic adj.

apprise v. To inform [of]. To notify. Make aware, tell, warn, advise, inform, communicate, notify, acquaint, give notice.

approbation n. Commendation, approval, recognition, praise. Approbatory adj.

atavistic adj. Characteristic of a throwback. Of or relating to reversion to a former or more primitive state. Regressive. Atavism n.

atrophy n. v. A wasting away through lack of use. To wither or shrink. Atrophic adj. Waste away, waste, shrink, diminish, deteriorate, decay, dwindle, wither, wilt, shrivel.

ban n. v. A prohibition. To prohibit. Block, restriction, veto, boycott, embargo, injunction, censorship, taboo, suppression, stoppage, disqualification, interdiction, interdict, proscription, disallowance.

conscientious adj. Governed by the dictates of conscience; principled. Conscientiously adv. Conscientiousness n.

culinary adj. Of or relating to a kitchen or to cooking.

deference n. adj. Courteous respect for the opinion, wishes, or judgment of another. Respect, regard, consideration, honor, esteem, courtesy, homage, reverence, politeness, civility, veneration, thoughtfulness. Deferential. adj.

detractor n. Defamer, libeler, critic, slanderer, disparager, traducer, vilifier, detract. v. Detraction n.

dilettante n. A dabbler pursuing superficially or amateurishly a few or many arts or fields of knowledge. Dilettantish adj. Dilettantism n.

draconian adj. Exceedingly strict, harsh or severe. Hard, stern, drastic, stringent, pitiless.

egregious adv. Conspicuously bad or objectionable. appalling, dreadful, shocking, notorious, horrific, outrageous, infamous, intolerable, monstrous, scandalous, frightful, heinous, abhorrent, insufferable.

emaciated adj. Extremely thin, undernourished. Skeletal, weak, lean, pinched, gaunt, atrophied, scrawny, attenuate, half-starved, cadaverous, macilent. Emaciate v.

enticement n. That which attracts by inspiring hope or desire. Bait, temptation, lure, allure, seduction, inducement, cajolery. Entice v.

eviscerate v. Disembowel, gut. Take away a vital or essential part of. Devitalise.

exorbitant adj. Exceeding all bounds. Flagrant, excessive, unreasonable, extravagant, immoderate.

fardel n. A pack, bundle or burden. Encumbrance, onus, load.

ineluctable adj. Unavoidable, inevitable, inescapable. Ineluctability n.

intrinsic adj. Of or relating to the essential nature of a thing. Inherent. native, built-in, underlying, congenital, inborn, inbred.

irreverence n. Lack of reverence or due respect. Desecration, profanation, sacrilege, blasphemy.

Kant Proper noun. German philosopher who sought to synthesize rationalism and empiricism.

laden adj. Weighed down with a load, loaded, encumbered, burdened. Hampered, weighted, full, taxed, oppressed, fraught. Load v.

laudation n. Praise, approval, acclaim, applause, tribute, ovation, accolade, panegyric, eulogy, commendation, approbation, acclamation, encomium, plaudit. Laud v.

mandate n. v. Command, order. Dictate, prescribe. Mandatory adj.

muse n. A source of inspiration. Any of the nine daughters of Mnemosyne and Zeus, each of whom presided over and inspired a different art or science. The muses are Calliope, Clio, Erato, Euterpe, Melpomene, Polyhymnia, Terpsichore, Thalia, and Urania.

obsolescent adj. Out of date. Vestigial.

polymath n. A person of great and varied learning. Polymathy n. Polymathic adj.

predilection [for] n. Proclivity. A partiality or disposition toward something; a preference. Bias, leaning, partiality, penchant, prejudice. propensity.

prenuptial adj. before marriage or a wedding.

prenuptial agreement n. A pact made before a marriage that determines how the estate of the couple is to be divided in the event of a divorce.

prerequisite n. adj. Required or necessary as a prior condition. Precondition, essential, necessity, imperative, requisite, sine qua non.

pretermission n. The act of disregarding or intentionally ignoring. Pretermit v.

prodigious adj. Imposingly great in size, force, or extent. Enormous, huge, giant, massive, vast, immense, gigantic, monumental, monstrous, mammoth, tremendous, colossal.

protestation n. A strong expression of dissent.

purported adj. Presumed to be, supposed.

reciprocal adj. Reflecting mutual action or relationship. An equal exchange or substitution. Quid pro quo. Exchange, interchange, tit for tat, equivalent, compensation, substitution.

reductionist n. One who attempts to explain a complex set of facts or phenomena by another, simpler set of component parts. Reductionism n.

remonstration n. Objection, protest, complaint, disagreement, dissent, remonstrance. Remonstrate v.

senile adj. Characteristic of old age. Geriatric, doddering, doting, in one's dotage, decrepit, faltering. Senility n.

stagnate v. To be or become stagnant. Characterized by lack of motion or vitality. Inaction, inactiveness, inactivity. Stagnant adj.

stigma n. A sign or mark of ignominy, disgrace or infamy. disgrace, shame, dishonor, stain, blot, reproach. Stigmal adj.

sumptuous adj. Characterized by splendor, suggesting great expense, lavish, resplendent, opulent.

superannuated adj. Outmoded, obsolete.

syndicated adj. Sold through a syndicate for publication or use in multiple venues or publications.

tort n. A wrongful act resulting in personal or property damage for which civil action may be taken. Wrongful conduct, misconduct, wrongdoing. Tortious adj.

tumult n. A disorderly commotion or disturbance. Disturbance, confusion, trouble, chaos, turmoil, turbulence, disorder, unrest, upheaval, havoc, mayhem, strife, disarray, ferment, agitation, bedlam. Tumultuous adj.

unrepentant adj. Exhibiting no remorse. Impenitent, remorseless.

upheaval n. A sudden, violent disruption or upset. Disturbance, revolution, disorder, turmoil, disruption, cataclysm, violent change.

vapid adj. Lacking taste, interest or flavor. Bland, insipid, unexciting, dull. Vapidity n.

Quiz

1. Boadicea
    A. aspired to be a dilettante
    B. wrote music for a prenuptial agreement
    C. intended to enter politics.
    D. brought an egg whisk to her uncle's wedding.

2. The prenuptial agreement
    A. was inedible.
    B. had curative powers.
    C. was sung without accompaniment.
    D. was written for the SCDI

3. The SCDI
    A. was stagnant.
    B. favored used textbooks.
    C. was founded by Boadicea.
    D. favored a ban on atrophy.

4. Boadicea's uncle Aloysius
   A. was vice president of the IDC
   B. owned an egg whisk.
   C. got married.
   D. sang in a choir.

5. The IDC
   A. was run by Boadicea's uncle Cuthbert.
   B. was atavistic.
   C. helped artists.
   D. inspired tumult and upheaval.

6. Core subjects at Stichwort
   A. were updated annually.
   B. were draconian.
   C. were out of date.
   D. were taught in Gujarati.

7. Textbook publishers representatives
   A. provided essay evaluation software.
   B. sang a cappella
   C. were the muses in Boadicea's painting.
   D. inspired tumult and upheaval.

8. The Unrepentant Recovering Reductionists
   A. occupied the office next to the SCDI.
   B. provided essay evaluation software.
   C. wore gaudy socks.
   D. was founded by Boadicea.

Answers

1. B.	5. A.
2. C.	6. C.
3. C.	7. D.
4. C.	8. A.

Language Notes

The World's Largest Usage Dictionary

Given a little practice and access to a networked computer, the writer can, with a few keystrokes and a few seconds, determine the correct usage of just about any word or phrase – much faster and with greater practical accuracy than by using any grammar or usage book.

The Oxford English Dictionary has long been the definitive place to find how a word has been used in literature. Many other dictionaries do not provide all of the information necessary to use a word confidently. However, when examples are needed and a quantity measurement of current web usage is required, search engines now provide an ideal resource. If, for example, one would like to know whether "normality" is more commonly used than Warren G. Harding's infamous "normalcy", one need only search them both and count their respective hits to discover that "normality" does in fact occur on the web with roughly twice the frequency of "normalcy". We have used the Google search engine in the examples below but other search engines should perform similarly and future search engines may provide many more options.

Searching for Usage on the Web

When uncertain about the use of a complete phrase or, for example, which preposition to use with a noun or verb, one can search the phrase in quotes. For example, "inclination to" is about seven times as commonly used as "inclination for", while "penchant for" is about 15 times as common as "penchant to".

It is usually possible to do a very specific search of online literature using a search engine to find the number of examples of a specific phrase that can be found on the web. It can be tricky to define the right search and one will almost always find erroneous usages, but in general, the quantity found on the web can justify a specific usage if one defines the search carefully and examines the context of the result.

For example, to determine which is correct "researches are" or "research is", a search for the two phrases (each in quotes) will yield a clear answer in the form of an approximate count of how many of each are found on the web (in our Google search: 210,000 and 17,300,000 respectively). If searched properly, the preponderant usage is nearly always safe to use. In some instances there may be grammar books that contend otherwise, but it's hard to take seriously the argument that prevailing usage is wrong.

Of course there will always be erroneous usages on the web (210,000 in the above example), and unusual contexts may result in spurious hits, but they are usually clearly outweighed by dominant usage.

One must be wary when using the search approach. Counting the wrong thing is perfectly possible, as in the case with verbs that form phrases with many different prepositions to mean many different things (take up, take over, take out, take down). This problem can usually be solved by examining the contexts of search results for usage and perhaps adding some context to the search phrase. But how does one get a representative sampling of such massive numbers as those above? There is one excellent way to do this with the help of certain search engine features. To reduce the search to a small sample and at the same time gain confidence in the usages found, one can restrict the search to specific countries, or domains.

Searching for Usage in Academic Sites

For example, searching on one occasion within the Cambridge University website, the Google search:
site://www.cam.ac.uk/ "researches are"
yielded no results at all, while
site://www.cam.ac.uk/ "research is"
yielded 28 hits. Had there been some question about the context of these phrases, it would be possible to look through those 28 examples fairly easily. One would also know that the source is highly trustworthy.

To search within a specific university domain, add
site:[url] (without the "http://")

For example:
site: www.cam.ac.uk/ "research is"
searches Cambridge university and
"research is" site:www.ox.ac.uk/
Would find instances of "research is" in Oxford University pages.

Limiting the search to a single university is usually an ideal solution for usage verification but in some cases, specifically very rare usages, it may be best to broaden the field. To do a Google search within a range of university sites, add this text to the search line with search term in quotes:

USA (and universities elsewhere): *site:.edu*

British universities: *site:.ac.uk*

Australian Universities: *site:.edu.au*

South African Universities: *site:.ac.za*

If one searches a common word and finds fewer than 10,000 hits, it can reasonably be assumed that it has been misspelled, but at the same time one is consoled with the knowledge of exactly how many web authors have misspelled the word precisely that way.

Preposition Matching and Collocation Searching

In the following quiz, a choice of propositions is presented for use in context and the instructions are to choose the correct one. Check your answers by searching them. (For example, search for "aversion from", "aversion to", "aversion over", "aversion about" and note the hit-count.)

Search examples from the following playsheet.

"plied about"	2,210
"plied with"	685,000
"plied over"	10,200
"plied from"	30,200

But for "laboring under" the results are less conclusive.

"laboring under"	816,000
"laboring over"	658,000
"laboring by"	20,300
"laboring about"	3,340

Sometimes, as in the above case, the choice may not seem clear. There are many ways for example that one might "labor over something. It might even be done with greater frequency than laboring under a misconception. In such cases, simply add more context.

"laboring under a misconception"	121,000
"laboring over a misconception"	37
"laboring by a misconception"	0
"laboring about a misconception"	0

Quiz: Preposition Matching and Searching Practice

Choose the correct preposition from the choices in square brackets. Check your answers using the strategies and examples above.

1. Boadicea plied Uncle Cuthbert [about, with, over, from] questions [about, with, over, from] his days as a member [for, from, of, on] the Ministry of Erroneous Assumptions (formed to dispel misconceptions [under, over, by, about] which members of the Ministry of Extraneous Folkloric Perversions had been laboring).

2. He stressed that his answer must be contingent [with, from, by, upon] receiving assurance that no member of the ministry be subjected [with, to, by, for] accusations of frivolity and general silliness nor would they be the subject [from, of, over, to] derisive mimicry including, but not limited to, verses, songs, chants, effigies, hand-puppetry, or other forms of demeaning comedic caricature.

3. Boadicea retorted that, though some ministers had diverged [on, in, from, for] the original fatuous agenda, in her opinion, complete reconciliation [with, over, by, onto] the Society for Conscientious Deferential Irreverence was unlikely while the ministry continued its present course. Indeed, five skits, a float, one song cycle, and a short oratorio had already been composed and significant progress had been made [around, in, on, by] costumes, scenery, and props, including a life-sized replica of a very baffled looking diplodocus.

4. Uncle Cuthbert interpreted Boadicea's response as the harbinger [of, for, from, over] a raucous and tumultuous weekend with members of the SCDI, redolent [from, of, with, over] curry, WD40, and decaying floral vegetation. He refrained [of, from, with, for] comment [for, of, with, by] fear that further remonstration might serve [as, for, with, by] inspiration -

something [from, over, with, by] which he was loathe to provide them.

5. Uncle Cuthbert has had an aversion [from, to, over, about] large incontinent rhinoceroses ever since the infamous incident with the hydrangea and the bag of infested Argentine lentils. He has even acquired a distaste [of, for, from, with] unsupervised pachyderms in any form though remains thoroughly enamored [about, for, from, of] wildebeest. He has always retained an inordinate fondness [of, for, with, about] water voles while never becoming fond [of, for, with about] mimes.

6. Aunt Agatha's views on waterfowl in the classroom diverge [to, from, with, for] those established by the provost, without whose avian predilections the campus would appear much like that of other colleges – but for the vast courtyard mosaics depicting farm machinery and turn-of-the-century diving equipment, on which score she finds little [from, on, with, to] which to disagree.

7. Pamela was indeed so in love [over, of, for, with] the hirsute aerialist that the audacious balloonist, [over, of, for, with] whom she had so recently been enamored, abandoned the cause and returned the diesel-powered vacuum cleaner and the hand-wrought Sicilian trivets.

Answers

Check answers using the searching methods presented above. When in doubt, always examine the context of search results. It is much more valuable to know how to determine the correct usage than to get the usage correct. In many cases, there is more than one correct option. For example, "redolent of" is about three times as common as "redolent with" yet both are used.

Remember: place each phrase in quotes. For example: "plied him about questions"
Common usages are boldfaced.

Context Searches:

1. plied him [about, **with**, over, from] questions
   questions [**about**, with, over, from] his
   was a member [for, from, **of**, on]
   laboring [**under**, over, by, about] misconceptions

2. be contingent [with, from, by, **upon**]
   be subjected [with, **to**, by, for]
   be subject [from, of, over, **to**]

3. diverge [on, in, **from**, for]
   reconciliation [**with**, over, by, onto] them
   progress made [around, in, **on**, by]

4. harbinger [**of**, for, from, over]
   redolent [from, **of**, **with**, over]
   he refrained [of, **from**, with, for] comment
   refrained [**for**, of, with, by] fear that
   might serve [**as**, for, with, by]
   provide them [from, over, **with**, by]

5. has an aversion [from, **to**, over, about]
   a distaste [of, **for**, from, with]
   be enamored [about, for, from, **of**]
   a fondness [of, **for**, with, about]
   was fond [**of**, for, with about].

6. views diverge [to, **from**, with, for] those
   little to disagree [from, on, **with**, to]

7. be in love [over, of, for, **with**]
   be enamored [over, **of**, for, with]

Projects

Rewrite *Boadicea Arrives on Stichwort Campus* in other words using the synonyms in the glossary for ideas.

Using words from the glossary:

1. Explain why Boadicea's Uncle Cuthbert was apprehensive about her coming to Stichwort.

2. Explain what the statue in the quad was demonstrating.

3. Describe your ideal college? What would the teachers be like? What would your ideal living accommodations be like? How many students should be in each class? What would the classes be like? What kind of tests would you prefer? What clubs or organizations would you want to belong to?

Chapter 2

Vocabulary: Baby Bear and the Yard Sculpture

Papa Bear's **sonorous** snore ceased suddenly as he awoke to find a **pugnacious** owl tugging at his ear.

sonorous adj. resounding
pugnacious adj. quarrelsome

"Flangia", he **remonstrated**. "What's the matter with you?"

remonstrate v. protest

"Your **puerile progeny** has again embarked on sculpting in the yard, this time it is not just **grotesque**, it is highly **redolent**."

puerile adj. childish
progeny n. offspring
grotesque adj. ugly
redolent adj. smelly

Upon rising, Papa Bear could not but sense the **fetid miasma** of something superbly **putrescent** wafting in the window, the which he shut with inspired **alacrity**. Still struggling with **vestigial somnolence**, he uttered a **sardonic** "Isn't the air fragrant this morning?"

fetid adj. unpleasant smelling
miasma n. evil vapor
putrescent adj. rotten
alacrity n. speed
vestigial adj. lingering
somnolence n. sleepiness
sardonic adj. bitingly sarcastic

Flangia retorted "Not a time for **banter**! It's wilting my geraniums."

banter n. teasing

Though doubtless **hyperbole**, Papa Bear did not attempt to **refute** the claim, preferring to respond with a **sagacious** "In adversity there is ever

hyperbole n. exaggeration
refute v. disprove

sagacious adj. wise

a **salutary** gem of **redemption** if one can find it."

"Oh, spare me the **platitudinous persiflage**. **Requisite** measures must be taken!"

Though by habit highly **indulgent**, when faced with the sight of the **festering edifice**, Papa Bear rubbed his nose in that special way which any who knew him would recognize as a **portent** of drastic action. They were joined by Mama Bear, an electric elk named Simon, and **sundry squamulose** distant relations, all **cognizant** of the **poignant gesticulation** and its significance.

Constructed from owl castings, all manner of **ordure, coprolite**, and **desiccated scatological residue**, the giant object of universal **repudiation** had already taken on an unmistakable likeness of Papa Bear himself.

He **couched** the reproof as an **aversion** to statuary in general, disregarding both subject matter and material used as irrelevant, though he did **decry** the **transient** nature of nontraditional media and the choice of medium for the subject.

---

salutary adj. healthy
redemption n. recovery

platitudinous adj. airy, overused
persiflage n. chatter
requisite adj. necessary
indulgent adj. tolerant
festering adj. rotting
edifice n. structure

portent n. omen

sundry adj. various
squamulose adj. scaly
cognizant adj. aware
poignant adj. moving
gesticulation n. gesture

ordure n. excrement
coprolite n. fossilized ordure
desiccated adj. dried up
scatological adj. relating to excrement
residue n. remainder
repudiation n. intense dislike
couch v. formulate
aversion n. dislike
decry v. condemn
transient adj. temporary

Glossary

alacrity adj. Speed; enthusiasm, readiness, promptness, rapidity.
Aversion [to] n. Dislike for; loathing [of], distaste [for],
    hatred [of]. Averse adj.
banter n./v. Repartee, wit, chitchat, mockery, teasing, persiflage.
cognizant [of] adj. Aware [of], conscious [of], vigilant,
    mindful [of]. Cognizance n.
coprolite n. Fossilized excrement.

couch [as] v. Formulate an utterance; express, phrase, imply.

decry v. Condemn, criticize, disparage, belittle, deprecate, vilipend.

desiccate v. Dry, dehydrate, parch. Desiccated adj.

edifice n. Structure, construction.

fetid adj. Unpleasant smelling; foul, putrid, rank, fusty.
   Fetidity n.

gesticulation n. A deliberate motion or gesture; expression, sign, signal, token. Gesticulate v. Gesticulatory adj.

grotesque adj. Bizarre, ugly, gross, monstrous, misshapen. Grotesque n. one that is grotesque. Grotesqueness n.

harbinger [of] n. One who or that which foreruns and announces the coming of any person or thing; portent, omen, foretokening, augury, herald.

hyperbole n. Extreme exaggeration; overstatement.
   Hyperbolic adj.

indulgent adj. Tolerant, non-judgmental, understanding, lenient. Indulgence n. Indulge v.

miasma n.   A noxious or poisonous atmosphere or influence; murk, pall. Miasmic adj. Miasmal adj. Miasmatic adj.

ordure n. Excrement, dung. Ordurous adj.

owl castings n.   Indigestible remnants of an animal devoured whole by an owl and later regurgitated.

persiflage n. Light or frivolous chatter. Banter.

platitude n. A written or spoken statement that is flat, dull, or commonplace; cliché, banality, insipidity.
   Platitudinous adj.

poignant adj. Severely painful or acute to the spirit; moving, emotional, touching, affecting. Poignancy n.

portent [of] n. Anything that indicates what is to happen; augury, foretokening, omen. Portend v. Portentous adj.

progeny n. Children, offspring, descendents.

puerile adj. Childish, juvenile, immature, callow.

pugnacious adj. Quarrelsome, confrontational, belligerent, truculent, contentious. Pugnacity n.

putrescent adj. Undergoing decomposition of animal or vegetable matter accompanied by fetid odors; rotting, decomposing. Putrescence n. Putrefy v.

redolent [of] adj. Having a strong odor; aromatic, fragrant, malodorous, stinking, smelly. Redolence n.

redemption n. Recovery; salvation, rescue, liberation. Redeem v.

refute v. To prove to be wrong; disprove, controvert, contest, deny, counter. Refutation n.

remonstrate v. Protest, object, reprove, complain. Remonstrance n. Remonstration n. Remonstrative adj.

repudiate v. To refuse to have anything to do with; reject, cast off, disclaim, disavow, renounce. Repudiation n.

requisite adj. Necessary, obligatory, mandatory, essential. n. Something that is indispensable; a requirement.

residue n. Remains, dregs, remainder. Residual adj.

sagacious adj. Able to discern and distinguish with wise perception; wise, sage, perceptive, erudite. Sagacity n.

salutary adj. Health inducing; beneficial, helpful, salubrious, constructive.

sardonic adj. Scornfully or bitterly sarcastic; scornful, mocking, derisive, satirical. Sardonicism n.

scatology n. The scientific study of feces. The chemical analysis of excrement (for medical diagnosis or for paleontological purposes). Scatological adj. Of or relating to excrement or its study.

somnolence n. Sleep, sleepiness, drowsiness. Somnolent adj.

squamulose adj. Covered with small scales; scaly, squamous.

sonorous adj. Resounding, resonant, booming, echoing, reverberating.

sundry adj. Various, mixed, miscellaneous.

transient adj. Of limited duration; fleeting, brief, temporary, momentary, transitory, ephemeral, evanescent. Transience n.

transient n. One who stays for only a short time; transitory, fleeting.

vestigial adj. Of or relating to a remaining or lingering trace of something previously present; residual, lingering, enduring, remaining. Vestige n.

Quiz

1. Flangia is
      A. an elk.   B. an owl.
      C. scaly.   D. an artist.

2. Papa Bear
      A. slept quietly.   B. flew into a rage.
      C. shut the window.   D. grew geraniums.

3. Papa Bear was
      A. wide awake.
      B. bored with sculpture.
      C. angry with Baby Bear.
      D. awakened by an owl.

4. Baby Bear's sculpture
      A. sculpted smelled like geraniums.
      B. was in the front yard.
      C. bothered an elk.
      D. was in granite.

5. _____ was normally indulgent.
      A. Papa Bear   B. Baby Bear
      C. Flangia   D. Simon

6. The festering edifice
      A. looked like Papa Bear.
      B. wilted geraniums.
      C. was a portent of drastic action.
      D. was highly appreciated.

7. Papa bear's rubbing his nose
      A. portended drastic action.
      B. indicated a powerful odor.
      C. could not be seen.
      D. irritated Flangia.

8. Some relations
   A. were redolent.
   B. were scaly.
   C. were colorful.
   D. wore gaudy socks.

9. Baby Bear
   A. opened the window.
   B. grew geraniums
   C. used non-traditional media.
   D. smelled bad.

10. The wilting of the geraniums
    A. portended drastic action.
    B. was hyperbole.
    C. was redolent.
    D. made Papa Bear close the window.

Answers

1. B
2. C
3. D
4. B
5. A
6. A
7. A
8. B
9. C
10. B

Language Notes

Common Errors: Singular and Plural

A subject and its verb must agree in number.

singular subject	he/she/it	The Munchkin	Rowland
plural subject	they	the Munchkins	Rowland and Boadicea

singular verb	is	was	has	walks
plural verb	are	were	have	walk

Correct:
he is, she is, the Munchkin was, Rowland has
they are, the Munchkins were, Rowland and Boadicea have

Incorrect:
he are, the Munchkins was, they was, Rowland and Boadicea has

Your ear can usually tell whether they agree: *He is (*not *he are), they were (*not *they was).* For complete rules of verb conjugation, see the Verb section of Appendix B (P241) . Most native speakers of English have a fairly good feel for subject/verb matching under normal circumstances and simply need to learn how to recognize unusual sentence constructs in order to apply their intuitive language sense. As usual, English has some unexpected traps for the unwary though.

Either/Neither

Normally either (or neither) is considered singular

Neither of them was aware of the impending flood of mayonnaise.

or

Neither the ox nor the wildebeest was found to look particularly decorative in the store window.

However, when one of the elements connected together with *either* is plural, the construct becomes plural **IF** it is the element closest to the verb.

Singular:

*Neither the purple bottles nor the turnip **was** quite the right shade of mauvy puce.*
("turnip" is singular)

However:

Plural:

*Neither the turnip nor the purple bottles **were** quite the right shade of mauvy puce.*
("purple bottles" is plural)

The Number/A Number

"The number" is singular
The number of amateur astronauts is fairly small.

"A number" is plural
A number of amateur astronauts were milling about and waving spoons.

Subject/verb agreement can also become tricky in more complex sentences and when the subject and verb are separated by extraneous material.

Wrong:

> *Rowland and Boadicea, when applying to the Clockwork Submarine Enthusiast' Amateur Operatic Society, was invisible behind the giant mushroom.*

Always start by identifying the subject and verb. Then bring them together and use your ear to determine if they sound right.

In this case, the subject is *Rowland and Boadicea* and the verb is *was*. It should be *Rowland and Boadicea were* because *Rowland and Boadicea* is a plural subject and must take the plural verb form *were*.

In the following examples, practice identifying subject and verb. Use them together to see if they match, and check your answers.

Quiz

1. The brown leeches, the only really appetizing items in the buffet, was hardly a substitute for bungee jumping in renaissance costume outside the embassy.

2. Rowland and Boadicea, of the Gypsy Violinists' Existential Reading Circle, was visibly distressed at the state of the herring tarts.

3. Neither Rowland nor Boadicea, when hiding from members of the Clockwork Submarine Enthusiast's Amateur Operatic Society, were visible behind the giant mushroom.

4. Quilp Springle, author of the monograph, *Romance Languages as a Primary Cause of Dental Deformities*, were unavailable for comment.

5. Neither the dwarf on his tricycle nor the accountants with their wheelbarrow was able to overtake the heavily laden swallow.

6. Neither of the flamingoes show any sign of plotting sedition.

7. The number of mistakes he made were limited only by his typing speed.

8. A number of variations on the painting, *The Muses Contemplating an Egg Whisk,* was up for auction as was a wealth of marginally bizarre and somewhat dangerous looking kitchen utensils.

Answers

1.

	subject	verb
wrong:	The brown leeches	was
correct:	The brown leeches	were

2.

	subject	verb
wrong:	Rowland and Boadicea	was
correct:	Rowland and Boadicea	were

3. **Note** that when either or neither links multiple subjects, the one closest to the verb is the one that determines how the verb is conjugated. In this case, Boadicea is singular and thus the verb should match a singular subject.

	subject	verb
wrong:	Neither Rowland nor Boadicea	were
correct:	Neither Rowland nor Boadicea	was

4.

	subject	verb
wrong:	Quilp Springle	were
correct:	Quilp Springle	was

5.   Again, when multiple subjects are linked with *neither* the one closest to the verb is the one that counts. In this case, *accountants* is plural and the verb must match: *the accountants were*.

	subject	verb
wrong:	Neither the dwarf nor the accountants	was
correct:	Neither the dwarf nor the accountants	were

6.   In this case, *neither* itself is the subject. *of the flamingoes* is simply a modifier. The word *neither* on its own is singular.

	subject	verb
wrong:	Neither	show
correct:	Neither	shows

7.   The word *number* is an interesting case. *The number* is singular, yet *a number* is plural.

	subject	verb
wrong:	The number	were
correct:	The number	was

8.   Again, the word *number* is an interesting case. *The number* is singular, yet *a number* is plural.

	subject	verb
wrong:	A number	was
correct:	A number	were

Verb Conjugation and Phrase Construction

Most native speakers have no problem conjugating verbs correctly, constructing verb phrases and choosing appropriate tenses, but many do have difficulty correctly identifying and describing verb phrases. The following verb phrase playsheet presents examples and simple sentences to practice on. ESL students and those who have problems with this are encouraged to refer to the verb section of appendix B which presents exhaustive rules for conjugation and verb phrase construction. (*See* Verb Conjugation Rules, p241 and Rules for Creating Verb Phrases in Perfect, Progressive, and Passive, p245)

Verb Phrase Playsheet

Convert the following sentences into perfect, progressive, and passive forms and combinations thereof.

Example: The segmented larva confuses Alice.

> *Perfect:* The segmented larva has confused Alice.

> *Progressive:* The segmented larva is confusing Alice.

> *Passive:* Alice is confused by the segmented larva.

> *Perfect Progressive:* The segmented larva has been confusing Alice.

> *Progressive Passive:* Alice is being confused by the segmented larva.

> *Perfect Passive:* Alice has been confused by the segmented larva.

> *Perfect Progressive, Passive:* Alice has been being confused by the segmented larva.

1. Aloysius beats the crotchety rhinoceros about the ears with his shoe.

2. Rupert hides the more dangerous office equipment under his bagpipes.

3. The erroneous taxonomic decision delights the mischievous monotreme.

4. Rupert teaches the irascible cat to whistle.

5. Boadicea tickles the sleeping dragon.

6. The magnetic banshee fears doorknobs and postcards.

7. The Egyptian archaeologist unearths what appears to be an ice cream scoop and a jar of pickled onions.

8. The performance combines curling, figure skating, and Irish dance.

9. Boadicea offers them the irradiated fruitcake and the mukluks.

10. The magistrate experiences highly flammable eructations.

11. The rodent infestation baffles the corpulent mayor.

12. Bewhiskered lagomorph seeks gloves and fan.

13. The caterpillar staunchly denies the insightful insinuation.

14. The three porcine siblings repel the lupine assault.

15. The king condemns the grinning feline.

16. The swagman prefers the stagnant billabong.

17. The 16 foot carnivorous marsupial pursues the hapless engine driver.

18. The misanthropic parking attendant brandishes a murderous miniature pikestaff.

19. The signet censured its singing sibling.

Archaic Usages

> *Upon rising, Papa Bear could not but sense the fetid miasma of something superbly putrescent wafting in the window, <u>the which</u> he shut with inspired alacrity.*

The definite article "the" is normally used to modify a noun, "the sniggering squirrel" for example. However, in the English of earlier periods it could be used to modify the relative pronoun "which" as in "the which he shut with inspired alacrity". By modern standards, this is a very peculiar usage and it can certainly be expected to elicit comment, consternation, or criticism from many English teachers if submitted in modern composition. Nonetheless, one should be able to expect and recognize it in literature:

> *... I put you to*
> *The use of your own virtues, for the which*
> *I shall continue thankful.* – Shakespeare,
> *All's Well that Ends Well*

Projects

Rewrite *Baby Bear and the Yard Sculpture* in other words using the synonyms in the glossary for ideas.

Using words from the glossary:

1. Explain why Flangia was upset and what she did.

2. Describe Papa Bear's reaction to the festering edifice.

3. Explain what Baby Bear was trying to do.

4. Describe a parental prohibition that upset you.

5. Describe a project you might consider that would put your house in an uproar.

Chapter 3

Vocabulary: Stichwort College Weathers the Storm

The Stichwort College administration was at a loss to find a way to justify removing the **satirical edifice** from the campus quad without losing face or providing Boadicea's SCDI with grounds for voicing righteous **umbrage**. Boadicea hoped they would hurry, for, as the **tome**-laden student had been erected in a rush almost overnight and was never expected to survive ensuing **disceptation**, the work was not intended to be particularly **durable** and was already showing signs of **disintegration**. The contention that it obstructed the view of the intersection, thus presenting a hazard to students from grounds and maintenance vehicles was posited and the SCDI dismantled it with only a **pro forma** complaint.

satire n. parody
edifice n. structure

umbrage n. offense
tome n. volume

disceptation n. controversy

durable adj. lasting
disintegration n. falling apart

pro forma adj. presented as a formality

The display had served its purpose. Professors had begun to ask the price of textbooks considered for adoption and were taking cost into account in the decision. Students had become aware that some classes could be taken without **extortionate** textbook requirements and flocked to them. The law of supply and demand that had been so **conspicuously** absent in the process had suddenly become a factor. Some professors even welcomed the excuse to create and provide their own class material and their efforts were duly noted and publicized, in part through the increasingly popular pamphlets of the SCDI whose membership was experiencing **unprecedented accretion**.

Other faculty members whose classes had suffered falling enrolment complained bitterly that their teaching responsibilities would become overwhelmingly **onerous** and oppressive without the **ancillary** material provided by textbook publishers and spoke of uniform enforcement of textbook adoptions. These (including the two who had availed themselves of Barbadian retreats the previous summer) were ignored for the **nonce** by the SCDI which had other problems to deal with.

extortionate adj. excessive

conspicuous adj. obvious

unprecedented adj. without
   prior example
accretion n. growth

onerous adj. burdensome
ancillary adj. secondary

nonce n. present

Scene: An office on the Stichwort campus. Dr. Hegemone is playing solitaire on the computer and quickly changes the screen to a spreadsheet after she hears a knock.

Characters: Dr. Hegemone, College Provost and Captain Uffisian, campus police.

Dr. H: Yes.
[Uff enters]
Uff: Good morning. You wanted to see me?
H: Yes Dorik. Have a seat. Have you read the latest one?
Uff: You mean the SCDI Rag? No. Was there another one today?
H: Yes of course there was another one today. You may not be able to stop it but you should at least know what they're doing.
Uff: Why? What are they doing?
H: We're both in it. Yes, not by name, but you can't miss us.
Uff: What?
H: You're a weasel in a Pickelhaube … a WW I German helmet.
Uff: What are you?
H: [...] that's not the point. Have you talked to them?
Uff: Yes of course. And Sgt. Melnik spent yesterday afternoon explaining the new regulations to them.
H: So what happened?
Uff: They offered him soup.
H: Soup?
Uff: Yes, some amazingly delectable soup from an ancient Greek recipe. He brought some back to the station.
H: Okay, Okay. What happened?
Uff: and they gave him a haircut.
H: [Simply glares at him and motions for him to keep going]
Uff: Well, they wrote a song about him. It's been playing on campus radio all morning.
H: Oh that's what that Melnik the Magnificent is about?
Uff: Yes.
H: So. [More heatedly] What did Melnik accomplish?
Uff. I'm really not quite sure. Mostly he just talked about the soup.
[Pause]

H: What have you been able to do about the fliers on campus?

Uff: We found a way to prohibit the posting of fliers just about everywhere on campus.

H: We can't do that with legitimate campus clubs.

Uff: Well, we can't prohibit their postings but we can prohibit posting on certain surfaces. It's never been permitted on painted surfaces and glass. We just added more things to the list: wood, metal, tile, plastic, composite, cinderblock. There are over 50 surfaces on the list now. We made sure there was nothing left for them to post on.

H: Why did I see that pink notice, the one with the tortoise and the baseball cap on the wall by the theater yesterday?

Uff: Don't worry. We've taken it down.

H: Did you take action against those who posted it?

Uff: We couldn't really do that.

H: Why not?

Uff: You may not have noticed, but, at some point, that wall has been repaneled.

H: Repaneled with what?

Uff: Linguine.

H: Linguine?

Uff: Yes. Not on the list I'm afraid. And beautifully done too.

H: Isn't that an actionable offense?

Uff: Paneling walls with linguine? Well no, not as such.

H: Okay, I'll see to it. [Writes] And the added security cameras?

Uff. Are due to be installed Friday.

H: What about the web page. We do control what appears under the college domain do we not? And that includes the SCDI site. Have you looked at what's there?

Uff: Have you looked closely at the domain name when you go to the SCDI page?

H: Uh, no. Why?

Uff: I talked to Geoff in IT. Their official site is just a forwarding splash page. Their domain name is just slightly different. And it seems that it's being hosted in Austria.

H: Austria?

Uff: Not much we can do.

H: We could at least turn off the link from our domain.

Uff: Geoff says nobody uses it uses it anymore. Everyone's blog links to it anyway and the URL is on all the fliers and pamphlets.

... I don't understand why they are so popular.

H: You haven't read it have you?

Uff: No, sorry. I don't read much. [H throws Uff a copy of a pamphlet].

H: Try. New experiences can be enlightening.

Uff:, [obviously a bit uncomfortable, starts laboriously to read.]

... and when confronted by the terrycloth squid ...

... breakfast to remember ...

... smoldering bagpipes ...

... waffle iron ...

[Turns a page, starts to giggle, laughs out loud, points at H, laughs again, dissolves into paroxysms of uncontrollable asphyxiating hilarity and writhes on the floor in spasms. H has been becoming visibly more irritated and ends up burying her face in her hands in despair.]

Small, black, sound-enabled security cameras suddenly appeared in public areas about the campus. Various student groups protested the potential threat to privacy that this form of **invigilation** might pose. Protests were mounted. Complaints were filed. Some of the more **militant** elements **advocated** vandalism.

invigilation n. proctoring

militant adj. combative
advocate v. endorse

In a hastily convened meeting of the SCDI which was suddenly being looked to as a **cynosure** by both more and less reputable members of the campus community, Boadicea strongly **abjured** militant action, maintaining that the development might well

cynosure n. example to
others

abjure v. reject

be a **propitious fortuity** in disguise. She called for the creation of "grikkles", an **ad hoc** art form she had invented that afternoon.

propitious adj. fortunate
fortuity n. chance event
ad hoc adj. improvised

The following Tuesday, at a scheduled rally in the quad, a platform was erected and a grikkle performed with hand puppets. The intimate audience in attendance was very impressed – as were the members of the campus police surveillance detail assigned to monitor the new cameras, directly in front of one of which the platform had been erected and the grikkle performed.

Highly inspired Grikkles were presented which rapidly became must-see watching among campus police, their mildly subversive and **seditious** subjects having been tailored to their intended audience. Boadicea seemed to have a clear picture of the reception they were getting, who was watching and how best to appeal to campus officers and cadets. Nobody doubted that some members of the campus **constabulary** had become sympathetic to the SCDI and its goals and were in communication with them.

seditious adj. subversive

constabulary n. police

The fact that each week's new grikkle was met with increased anticipation among campus police and attracted a **pullulative** crowd around the surveillance monitors eventually became

pullulative adj. swarming

known to the administration when Uncle Cuthbert paid a visit to the station to investigate community complaints of campus police vehicles illegally parked across multiple parking spaces at the local doughnut shop. Provost Hegemone became concerned that the SCDI was having undue influence upon the cadets and forbade watching the main quad monitor. Then, after grikkles were presented for various other cameras, watching the monitors was forbidden altogether.

It was pointed out in the faculty senate, (having been the subject of caricatures in the next grikkle) that the investment in surveillance equipment was a bit pointless if monitoring was prohibited. Shortly thereafter, surveillance details were resumed with the sound feed disabled.

Reducing the surveillance detail to watching hand puppetry **pantomimes** did not endear the administration to members of campus law enforcement who had then to resort to watching the grikkles online on their own time. Boadicea had acquired another audience and new allies.

pantomime n. storytelling without words, using gestures.

The following week, campus police resumed their long-standing efforts to acquire video and game players in the break lounge.

Glossary

abjure v. Recant, renounce, eschew, repudiate, reject, forswear, retract, disown. Abjuration n.

accretion n. Augmentation by gradual external addition. Growth, increase, addition, expansion, supplementation, proliferation, accumulation, enlargement, increment, waxing. Accretionary, accretive adj.

ad hoc adj. Devised for a single purpose. Improvisatory, extemporaneous, impromptu, unrehearsed.

advocate [for] v. To speak, plead, or argue in support of. Recommend, endorse, champion, propose, favor, defend, promote, urge, advise, justify, campaign for, commend, espouse, countenance. Advocate n. Advocation n. Advocative adj.

ancillary adj. Supplemental, of secondary importance. Having the characteristics of an added item, such as a workbook provided to support a textbook. Supplementary, additional, subsidiary, accessory, subordinate, auxiliary, contributory. Ancillary n.

conspicuous adj. Evident, visible, easy to notice, obvious, clear, apparent, manifest, noticeable, blatant, discernible, salient, perceptible.

constabulary n. A police force. The officers in a police force collectively as a group. Gendarmerie. Constable n.

cynosure n. That which serves as a source of attention, admiration and influence. A guide. Counseling, guidance, counsel, direction. Cynosural. adj.

disceptation n. Controversy, argument, contention, altercation, argumentation.

disintegration [pf] n. Loss of cohesion or unity. Reduction to pieces, fragments. Decomposition, fragmentation, decay. Disintegrate v.

durable adj. Capable of withstanding wear and tear. Resistant to decay or erosion. Lasting, strong, tough, sound, substantial, reliable, sturdy. Durability n.

edifice n. A building, especially one of imposing appearance or size. An elaborate conceptual structure. Building, house, structure, construction. Edificial adj.

extortionate adj. Exorbitant, gouging, excessively expensive, usurious, outrageous, steep, unconscionable, immoderate. Extort v. Extortion n.

fortuity n. A chance occurrence or event. Coincidence, happenstance. Fortuitous adj.

invigilation n. Proctoring [an examination]. Surveillance, superintendence, supervising, supervision, oversight. Invigilate v.

militant adj. Of combative or confrontational nature. Inimical, acrimonious, rancorous, refractory, contumacious, aggressive, warring, fighting, belligerent. Militance, militancy n.

nonce n. [for the nonce] The present or particular occasion. [For the] present. [For the] time being.

onerous adj. Troublesome or oppressive, distasteful, burdensome, trying, hard, taxing, demanding, difficult, heavy, crushing, exhausting, troublesome, oppressive, laborious, irksome, backbreaking, exigent.

pantomime n. Storytelling without words, using only bodily movements, gestures, and facial expressions. Pantomimic adj. Pantomimist n.

Pro forma Presented as a formality, perfunctory. To be used for a single purpose.

propitious adj. Favorable, desirable, auspicious. Timely, promising, opportune, fortunate, encouraging, bright, lucky, prosperous, rosy, advantageous.

pullulative adj. Tending to breed or increase in number rapidly or abundantly. Swarming, teeming, seething. Pullulate v. Pullulation n.

satire n. Parody, mockery, caricature, spoof (informal), travesty, lampoon, skit. Satirical adj. Satirist n.

seditious adj. Rebellions against the authority of a state. Inciting public disorder, revolutionary. Rabble-rousing, treasonous, subversive, disloyal. Sedition n.

tome n. A book, especially a large or scholarly one. One book in a series of volumes.

umbrage n. [to take umbrage] A feeling of anger caused by being
offended. Offense, anger, resentment.
unprecedented adj. Having no previous example. Unparalleled,
unheard-of, singular, exceptional, new, unusual, original,
novel, abnormal, ground-breaking. Precedent n.

Quiz

1. Boadicea
    A. wanted an excuse to take down the statue.
    B. took umbrage at the decision to remove the statue. .
    C. wore a Pickelhaube.
    D. needed a haircut.

2. The statue of the student with the pack of books
    A. symbolized the irrelevance of course offerings.
    B. had curative powers.
    C. was dismantled by campus police.
    D. was not made to last.

3. Sgt. Melnik
    A. was given soup by the Kantian Culinary Creationists.
    B. wore a Pickelhaube.
    C. wanted an excuse to take down the statue.
    D. had a song written about him.

4. According to Dr. Hegemone,
    A. linguine was acceptable construction material.
    B. the SCDI had been gardening without due care and at-
    tention.
    C. Dorik was caricatured in the SCDI pamphlet.
    D. Captain Uffisian was a weasel.

5. The posting of fliers on campus
    A. required a permit from the IDC.
    B. was permitted only on painted surfaces.
    C. was extremely tasteless and rebarbative.
    D. was prohibited on glass.

6. Captain Uffisian
    A. was bitingly sarcastic.
    B. conferred with Geoff in IT.
    C. loved the soup but disliked the linguine.
    D. was not amused by the SCDI pamphlet.

7. The Society for Conscientious Deferential Irreverence
    A. protested to installation of security cameras on campus.
    B. was looked to for guidance by disreputable elements on campus.
    C. had its website hosted in Australia.
    D. gave Captain Uffisian a haircut and a manicure.

8. Grikkles were
    A. acceptable places to post fliers.
    B. not permitted outside the cafeteria.
    C. a hastily devised art form for a specific purpose.
    D. often eaten for their negative calorie content.

9. Hand puppetry pantomimes
    A. were used to promote soup.
    B. were what grikkles became when viewed with the sound feed turned off.
    C. had a soothing effect upon less reputable elements on campus.
    D. had a pullulative effect.

10. Hand puppetry pantomimes
    A. demonstrated the irrelevance of courses.
    B. were disappointing to campus law enforcement.
    C. were performed with linguine.
    D. prompted the administration to turn off the camera sound feed.

Answers

1. A.	6. B.
2. D.	7. B.
3. D.	8. C.
4. C.	9. B.
5. D.	10. B.

Language Notes

Articles

An article is generally required for singular nouns in English, though as we will see, there are many exceptions to this rule. The indefinite article ("a" or "an" depending on whether the following word starts with a vowel) precedes the noun when the particular instance of that noun is undetermined, when it is simply "any" [noun] "A man in a hat regarded the blue object with curiosity." The definite article, "the", is normally used when one specific case of a noun is meant: "The dinosaur I saw had longer eyelashes than yours." But it can also signify an iconic or representative abstraction: "To the researcher, such events can be very revealing. To the random vacationer, they are simply irritating." (No specific researcher or vacationer is referred to here, only researchers and vacationers in general.)

Normally, singular nouns require an article, while plural nouns take no article if indefinite, "people are funny", or a definite article if a specific group of the noun is meant. "The people who planned the ice-cream barrage are in this room." There are some general rules, but also many exceptions which simply have to be learnt, and the British and Americans don't agree on everything.

Dictionaries and other reference resources rarely explain whether a noun needs an article or not. While there is no irrefragable rule, there are some guidelines. With some nouns, particularly place names and proper nouns, there is no consistent rule. Correct usage can only be learnt from experience or by looking them up which is often best done using a web search. It is ***The*** *San Joaquin Valley*, ***The*** *Rift Valley* and ***The*** *Holme Valley*, but *Death Valley*, *Grass Valley*, and *Apple Valley* don't take an article. This aspect of English can be very confusing to those unfamiliar with a region.

It might seem that the statistical web search devices used with collocation and verb phrases would solve the problem handily but it's not quite that simple. Let's take two examples: The Mississippi Valley and Death Valley – one which takes an article and one which doesn't. Searching for instances of "The Mississippi Valley" and "The Death Valley" is easy, but how does one search for instances of "Mississippi Valley" without the "the"? This can actually be done by using the exclude feature of the search engine. In Google, putting a "-" (a hyphen or minus sign) before an item eliminates any results containing that item. Thus, a search for

"Mississippi Valley" –"The Mississippi Valley"

will return only those pages that contain "Mississippi Valley" without the "the". However, this doesn't entirely solve the problem.

When used as a proper noun, those nouns that need an article will have one, but when the valley is used as an adjective, the presence or absence of an article in front of it is meaningless as it would be determined not by the valley but the noun it modifies:

Mississippi Valley dogwood species,

Mississippi Valley itinerant disk jockeys,

Mississippi Valley special-needs library assistants,

The Mississippi Valley dogwood species,

The Mississippi Valley itinerant disk jockeys,

The Mississippi Valley special-needs library assistants

Although this fact will certainly skew the count, it does not prevent the use of demotic search statistics to determine Web usage. It just means that the numbers may not tell the whole story and that some quick context examination may be needed. Usually, searching within a few educational sites and examining the results is sufficient. In most cases, the count will still probably be a reliable measure as spurious instances of the presence and absence of an article for the following noun will most likely be fairly randomly divided and will cancel each other out. Experiment.

Exceptions to the Rule Requiring Articles for Singular Nouns in English

In certain contexts, particularly in advertisements limited to a certain number of words, articles tend to be omitted altogether:

- Student seeks diesel powered saxophone.

- Wanted: flat with room for motorscooter and trebuchet.

- For sale: slightly used Etruscan trivet with certificate of authenticity.

Names of countries have no articles (if singular)

- France borders Switzerland.

- The BBC is not permitted in Zimbabwe.

- But: (plural country names) I'm visiting the United States next week after touring the Netherlands and the British Isles.
- Exceptions: I have never been to **the** Ukraine, **the** Gambia, nor **the** United Kingdom (or **the** UK).

There is no article used with the names of languages.

- My Swedish was not much use in Argentina.
- English has a vast vocabulary.
- Mahatma Gandhi corresponded in Gujarati.

There is no article before the names of meals.

- Breakfast was revolting.
- We had lunch with a dyspeptic Croat.
- Dinner only started to get interesting after midnight when Rupert revealed his sandwich.

There is no article with proper names (if singular).

- Rupert dropped the eggplant on the Persian carpet.
- Geoffrey bent his spanner stirring the porridge.
- But: (plural) the Morgans have novel table manners (plural proper noun).
- Exceptions: **The** Fonz, **the** Cisco Kid, **the** Scarlet Pimpernel.

There is no article with titles and names:

- Prince Charles has big ears.
- President Fillmore is the one nobody remembers.
- Dr. House insulted the patient.
- But: **the** Prince of Wales, **the** Bishop of Canterbury, and **the** Dalai Lama walked into a bar.

There is no article with professions and fields of study.

- Statistics is sometimes useful for proving things that aren't true.
- Music is rarely studied by the deaf.
- He put the finishing touches on his clown costume before interviewing with NASA.
- Mr. Murdstone would probably end up in food service or law enforcement.
- Exceptions: He'll probably end up in **the** military|**the** navy|**the** army.

There is no article with mass (uncountable) nouns:

- Water is rarely good for circuitry.
- Coffee can be used to disrupt a concert.
- Research is lacking in the field of invertebrate alcoholism.

There is no article with singular islands, mountains and lakes.

- More people know that Loch Ness doesn't have a monster than know that it isn't in Wales.
- Kauai is mostly coastline.
- Mount Fuji is the most photographed mountain in the world.
- Mussorgsky didn't name it "Pandemonium on Bald Mountain".
- But: The elephants traversed the Alps|the Pennines|the Adirondacks (plural).
- Exceptions: They climbed **The** Matterhorn. They went boating on **The** Serpentine. The dragon flew over **The** Lonely Mountain. **The** Hebrides is off the West coast of Scotland.

No article is used with geographical states, counties or subregions.

- She flew over Texas, Yorkshire, Bavaria, Tuscany and Queensland.

- Exceptions: **The** Transvaal is in South Africa.

No article is used with most names of towns, streets, stations and airports.

- Can you direct me to Curzon Street?

- She found joy in Sienna with a truculent balloonist.

- They depart from LAX on the 14th with far more empty liniment bottles than an expedition to Portugal normally requires.

- Charing Cross station is some distance from Piccadilly | Big Ben | Hyde Park Corner | St. Paul's Cathedral — but it's not close to: **the** Marble Arch | **the** Embankment | **the** London Eye | **the** Serpentine.

No article is used with some destinations:

- He went to school unwillingly. (He is in school.)

- She didn't go to work today. (She is at work.)

- They never went to college. (She is at college.)

- He might have gone to prison. (He is in prison.)

- They never go to church. (They are in church.)

- It's too early to go to bed. (He is in bed.)

- That's in skid row.

- They told us we were going to heaven or hell.

- She had to go to hospital (UK). But: she had to go to the hospital (USA).

Some nouns may be used with or without an article, but have very different meanings depending upon whether an article is used.

- She loves to walk in nature (the natural world). But, it is not **the** nature of cats to follow the herd (not characteristic of cats)

The article is absent in modes of transport and some expressions. Note significant differences between USA and UK usages.

We went:

- by car.
- by train.
- by air.
- on foot.
- on holiday (UK) on vacation (USA).
- on air. (in broadcasting)(UK) But: on the air (USA).

Projects

Rewrite *Stichwort College Weathers the Storm* in other words using the synonyms in the glossary for ideas.

Using words from the glossary:

1. Explain why Boadicea was anxious about leaving the statuary standing.

2. Write a skit using members of your family or school. Try to make their language consistent with what you would expect them to say.

3. Who is your favorite person in the story and the skit? Why?

Chapter 4

Vocabulary: Baby Bear and the Big Cheese

After finishing his porridge, Baby Bear resolved to spend the day upon a new artistic creation, his previous efforts at organic sculpture having been demolished and composted by his father despite his **impassioned** pleas and artful **perspicuity**. The argument had been that the nontraditional medium used was inappropriate for the subject matter. He viewed this contention as **specious, spurious** and **duplicitous**, suspecting the real motive to have been inspired by fundamental artistic differences – hitherto a bastion of **sacrosanctity** in the Bear household. He needed a new medium, one in keeping with his own **predilections** and at the same time generally acceptable.

impassioned adj. emotional
perspicuity n. eloquence

specious adj. unfounded
spurious adj. false
duplicitous adj. deceitful

sacrosanctity n. sacredness

predilection n. inclination

It must be noted that Baby Bear's concept of acceptable media may have been somewhat flawed. The medium he decided upon was cheese, and the subject was to be his mother. It would be a surprise, an **adulatory effigy** in fermented curd, and its configuration and **symmetry** were already forming in his mind's eye. There was a **profu-**

adulatory adj. reverent
effigy n. sculpture
symmetry n. balance

sion of cheeses about, an abundance due in no small part to his mother's **inordinate penchant** for the dairy product. Though a preference was not necessarily **endemic** to bears in general, she had long since **succumbed** to its allure and was, in fact, on **medication** for this condition. Thus it was not hard to fathom why he felt cheese would **fadge** best with his chosen subject, but the **convoluted** logic by which he came to the conclusion that this medium would be appropriate and acceptable and would not be viewed as a further act of **turpitude** was clear only to him.

He set immediately to work on a **furtive** collection campaign, storing wheels and blocks of cheese under his bed. His initial cache having been **spontaneously** augmented periodically by **opportunistic** acquisitions, after a week or so his bed tilted at an unconventional angle and began to bulge. **Undaunted**, he continued until sleeping in it became difficult and even hazardous.

He knew that, lest his plan be **subverted**, he needed to find a studio and start to work. Unfortunately, nothing presented itself. He was determined not to spoil the surprise, though perhaps his unwillingness to ask for help was more due to the **turmoil** and **discord** that would **ineluctably** disturb

---

profusion n. abundance
inordinate adj. excessive
penchant n. fondness of

endemic adj. natural to
succumb v. yield to
medication n. medicine

fadge v. to suit
convoluted adj. complicated

turpitude n. depravity

furtive adj. secret

spontaneous adj. unplanned
opportunistic   adj.   taking
    immediate advantage

undaunted adj.   not discou-
    raged

subvert v. destroy

turmoil n. state of agitation
discord n. disagreement
ineluctable adj. unavoidable

the serenity of the household **subsequent** to a revelation of his plans.

subsequent adj. after

To a **prodigy** such as Baby Bear, this was but a minor obstacle. His bed had gradually settled down again as the weather became warmer and the cheese relaxed into a less **rigid** structure. Palette knife in hand, he set about to fashion the mass into ... into what? — into something that would not arouse suspicion. Papa Bear did not at first notice the small piano in the corner of the kitchen the following morning but Baby Bear knew better than to expect his mother to overlook it. By the time she made an appearance the piano had vanished (but for a few greasy stains) and a small lumpy looking sofa had appeared on the veranda **supplanting** the chair that had stood there previously.

prodigy n. genius

rigid adj. unbending

supplant v. replace

When **queried** about the object, Baby Bear first **evaded** the question and eventually simply **disavowed** any knowledge of the misshapen object. Then, waiting for an **opportune** moment, he attempted to reshape the increasingly **redolent** mass into a microwave oven, an entertainment center, and eventually, a birdcage.

query v. ask
evade v. avoid
disavow v. deny

opportune adj. favorable

redolent adj. smelly

The **heterogeneity** of widely differing cheese **viscosities** rendered sculpting

heterogeneity n. quality of being composed of diverse elements
viscosity n. thickness

difficult, a fact to which Baby Bear attributed the utter lack of success achieved in these latter efforts.

Taking advantage of a few minutes alone in the living room, Baby Bear sculpted a likeness of his mother on the mantelpiece – or mostly on, for some oozed along the ledge and much dripped and dangled **pendulously** down in front of the fireplace.

pendulous adj. drooping

Upon its discovery, amid a **profusion** of **agitated deprecation** from both parents, was revealed a begrudging appreciation for his artistic vision and an acknowledgement of the **verisimilitude** in the explanation of his motivation.   With some **pomp** and a wheelbarrow, the bust was transported to the compost pile.   Another great project was already **festering** in his **fecund cranium**, but he resolved to embark on the next installment of his **cadent** accomplishments only after the house returned to its customary state of **tranquility**.

profusion n. large quantity
agitated adj. disturbed
deprecation n. scorn

verisimilitude n. appearance
   of truth
pomp n. showy display

fester v. decay
fecund adj. fertile
cranium n. head
cadent adj. regularly repeating
tranquility n. quiet repose

Glossary

abundance [of] n. Profusion, plenty, wealth. Abundant adj.

adulate v. To praise or admire excessively; fawn on, flatter, elevate, worship. Adulatory adj. Adulation n.

agitate v. Disturb, excite, perturb, trouble, disconcert. Agitation n. Agitated adj.

augment v. To make something greater, larger, or more extensive; enlarge, expand, enhance. Augmentation n.

cadent adj. Having cadence or rhythm; regularly repetitive. Cadence n.

configuration [of] n. Arrangement of parts or elements; relationship. Configure v.

controversy n. A dispute between parties holding opposing views; disagreement, debate. Controversial adj.

conventional adj. In accordance with general consensus or practice; predictable. Convention n.

convoluted adj. Having numerous overlapping folds; Intricate, complicated, elaborate complex. Convolution n. Convolute v.

cranium n. The part of the skull enclosing the brain; head, brain-case.

daunt v. To curtail the courage of; discourage, dismay, deter, dispirit, dishearten. Daunting adj.

deprecation n. Expression of disapproval;   condemnation, contempt, scorn, disparagement, opprobrium. Deprecate v. Deprecatory adj.

disavow v. To disclaim responsibility for; deny, renounce, disown. Disavowal n.

discord n. Tension or strife resulting from a lack of agreement; dissension, disagreement, conflict, friction. Discordant adj.

disheveled adj. Tousled, unkempt, untidy. Dishevelment n.

duplicity n. Double-dealing; deceit, deception, disloyalty. Duplicitous adj.

effigy n. Image, figure, carving, model, statue, sculpture.

endemic adj. Peculiar to some specified country or people; prevalent. Endemism n.

evade v. To escape or avoid; dodge, skirt. Evasive adj. Evasion n.

fadge v. To suit, match, or be appropriate. To fit with.

fecund adj. Fertile, prolific, fruitful, nubile.

fester v. To undergo decay, esp. in a wound; inflame, infect, corrupt, irritate, aggravate.

heterogeneous adj. Composed of elements with different properties; varied, assorted, various, mixed, non-uniform, dissimilar. Heterogeneity n.

impassioned adj. Imbued with passion; emotional, fervent, passionate. Impassion v.

incidental adj. Occurring as an unpredictable or minor side effect. Incident n.

ineluctable adj. Inevitable, unavoidable, inescapable, inexorable, indisputable. Ineluctability n.

inordinate adj. Excessive, unwarranted, extravagant. Inordinacy n.

medicate v. To treat with medicine; dose. Medication n.

medication n. Medicine, drug, prescription. Medicate v.

opportune adj. Suited or right in space and time; fitting, appropriate, favorable. Opportunity n. Opportunistic adj.

opportunistic adj. Taking immediate advantage of opportunities.

penchant [for] n. Inclination [to, for], proclivity [for, to], affinity [for, to], predilection [for], fondness [for].

pendulous adj. Hanging, swinging, depending, drooping.

periodic adj. Having or marked by repeated cycles; episodic, intermittent, sporadic, cadent. Periodicity n.

perspicuity n. Eloquence, lucidity, articulacy.

pomp n. Dignified or magnificent display; splendor, display, showiness, ceremony. Pompous adj. Pomposity n.

prodigy n. A person with exceptional talents or powers for a particular age; genius, phenomenon.

profuse adj. Plentiful; copious, abundant, generous, bountiful. Profusion n.

query v. To ask or question. Query n. A question.

redolent [of] adj. Having a strong odor; aromatic, fragrant, malodorous, stinking, smelly. Redolence n.

rigid adj. Incapable of or resistant to bending; inflexible, stiff, firm, unyielding. Rigidity n. Rigidify v.

sacrosanctity n. Quality of being sacred or sacrosanct.

serene adj. Unaffected by disturbance; calm, unruffled, tranquil, peaceful, unruffled. Serenity n.

specious adj. Baseless, erroneous, unfounded, false. Speciousness n. Speciosity n.

spontaneous adj. Arising from inherent qualities or tendencies without external cause; unprompted, unplanned, impulsive. Spontaneity n.

spurious adj. False, bogus, fake, counterfeit, imitation, unauthentic.

subsequent [to] adj. Following; succeeding, ensuing, successive, consequent, after.

subvert v. To destroy completely; ruin, undermine, threaten, destabilize. Subversion n. Subversive adj.

succumb [to] v. To cease to resist; yield, submit, surrender.

supplant v. To usurp the place of; displace, supersede, replace.

symmetry n. Exact correspondence of form on opposite sides of a
    dividing line or plane or about an axis point; regularity,
    balance, equilibrium. Symmetrical adj.
tranquil adj. Peaceful calm serene restful. Tranquility n.
    Tranquilize v.
turmoil n. A state of extreme agitation; commotion, tumult, confu-
    sion, mayhem.
turpitude n. Depravity, baseness, vulgarity.
verisimilitude n. The quality of appearing to be true or real. Veri-
    similitudinous adj.
viscosity n. Resistance (in a liquid) to flowing; thickness, stick-
    iness, glueyness, tackiness. Viscous adj.

Quiz

1. Baby Bear's previous organic sculpture
    A. was made in cheese.
    B. stood on the mantelpiece.
    C. was composted.
    D. was done in oatmeal.

2. Baby Bear's mother
    A. was the subject of his yard sculpture.
    B. disliked cheese.
    C. was on medication.
    D. found the piano in the kitchen.

3. Cheese
    A. was hard to find in the house.
    B. made Baby Bear's bed bulge.
    C. was used in Baby Bear's yard sculpture.
    D. was always sought after by bears.

4. Baby Bear created _____ out of cheese.
    A. a sewing machine   B. gaudy socks
    C. a piano   D. a waffle iron

5. Baby Bear's bed
    A. was made of cheese.
    B. tilted at an unconventional angle.
    C. was actually a waffle iron.
    D. was the subject of controversy.

6. Baby Bear sculpted with
    A. a waffle iron.   B. a palette knife.
    C. a spurtle.   D. a cheese grater.

7. A cheese sofa stood
    A. on the veranda.   B. in the kitchen.
    C. in the yard.   D. on the mantelpiece.

8. Baby Bear felt the birdcage was hard to sculpt
    A. because some cheeses were softer than others.
    B. because the cheese was too warm.
    C. because the cheese smelled strangely.
    D. because Mama Bear was on medication for cheese addiction.

9. The bust
    A. depicted Papa Bear.
    B. dripped on the sofa.
    C. evoked criticism.
    D. did not fadge with its subject.

10. The cheese was increasingly
    A. malodorous.   B. moldy.
    C. hard to find.   D. knurly.

Answers

1.	C	6.	B
2.	C	7.	A
3.	B	8.	A
4.	C	9.	C
5.	B	10.	A

Language Notes

Commonly Confused Verb Pairs

Lay and Lie

Even native speakers of English have trouble distinguishing between certain verb pairs which share forms and meanings, the most commonly misused probably being *lie* and *lay*.

A transitive verb takes an object. *Lay* is a transitive verb: *I lay the offensive soufflé before the embittered in-laws.* The verb *lay* acts directly upon a person or thing, in this case the soufflé, which is the object of the verb.

By contrast, the verb *lie* is intransitive. It takes no object and indicates the state of its subject: *The soufflé lies before the embittered in-laws.* The soufflé is the subject and the verb *lie* gives its state. English has several pairs of verbs that act this way, one transitive and the other intransitive. It is easier to recognize the differences between them by considering the present, past, and past participle forms of each.

Lie/Lay

present	past	past participle
lay	laid	laid
lie	lay	lain

Transitive: *Today I lay the soufflé before the embittered in-laws. Yesterday I laid it before the embittered in-laws. I have laid it before the embittered in-laws.*

Intransitive: *Today the soufflé lies on the table. Yesterday it lay on the table. It has lain on the table since September when it was still marginally edible.*

The *lie/lay* pair is particularly confusing as the past tense of the verb *lie* (*lay*) is the same as the present tense of the verb *lay*.

Other Oft-Mangled Pairs

Fell/Fall

present	past	past participle
fell	felled	felled
fall	fell	fallen

He fells a tree and the tree falls. Yesterday he felled the tree and the tree fell. The fallen tree was felled by a felonious furry fellow who fells firs that fall fast.

Raise/Rise

present	past	past participle
raise	raised	raised
rise	rose	risen

Raise the flag so they can see it rise above the landfill. When it rose, they could not understand why it would be raised where none had ever risen before.

She is raising a rose to rise higher than any other rose raised here has risen.

She rose late again today and then raised the issue of installing a luminous sundial for use before the sun has risen.

Hang/Hang

present	past	past participle
hang	hanged	hanged
hang	hung	hung

The verb *hang* is a special case in that the older transitive verb *hang/hanged/hanged* fell into disuse and survived only through being used as a legal term for execution by hanging, while *hang/hung/hung* has come to be used in all other senses, both transitive and intransitive. (The equivalent verbs in German are still used in their full transitive and intransitive forms: *hängen, hängte, gehängt* and *hangen hing gehangen.*)

Transitive: *They wanted to hang him today for rustling, but that was pointless as they already hanged him yesterday. They have hanged several rustlers, confiscated their potato chips, and threatened to hang one passerby who produced excessive noise with an eel skillet and a runcible spoon.*

Intransitive: *Today the revolting image hangs on the wall. Yesterday it hung on the wall. It has hung on the wall, evoking revulsion, for years.*

Note that, in each of these pairs, the transitive verb is regular, taking *ed* for its past and participial forms (except for *laid,* which has mutated a bit from *layed*), while the intransitive verb is irregular.

Lie / Lay Playsheet

Circle the errors in the following and correct them.

1. Could you lie those Etruscan water skis over there next to where the experimental begonias and the enigmatic Siberian banana sculpture are laying?

2. I couldn't rise the somnolent tortoise high enough to be seen above the rising flood of enthusiastic insipient herpetologists.

3. I couldn't figure out whether to fall or fell the tree before it falls on its own, so I just cut it down.

4. Tiberius couldn't sit the elaborate but somewhat aging eggplant centerpiece so that it would set reliably upright on the table, so he lay it down next to the infuriated Rabbi.

5. The imaginary emu lay in the corner of the room blithely laying eggs and knitting thneeds.

6. Set it on the couch beside the tureen where the querulous scabiosa is laying and the truculent eschscholtzia is setting.

7. I couldn't lie down where the peacock had laid yesterday.

8. I couldn't lie down where the peahen had laid yesterday.

Answers

1. The transitive verb "lay" is required to do anything to the water skis: "Could you lay those Etruscan water skis…".

2. The transitive verb "raise" is needed to raise the tortoise.

3. Here "fell the tree" would be correct if it won't fall on its own.

4. One must "set" (transitive) a centerpiece so it will "sit" (intransitive) reliably upright. He "laid" (transitive) it down.

5. No error. "lay" is the past tense of the intransitive "lie" – exactly what an imaginary emu would do in a corner. The transitive "lay" is the appropriate verb to describe an oviparous animal (even an imaginary one) producing eggs.

6. Set ("set" is correctly transitive) it on the couch beside the tureen where the querulous scabiosa is "lying" (intransitive) and the truculent eschscholtzia is "sitting" (intransitive).

7. "Lie" is correctly intransitive: "I couldn't lie down". The peacock had however "lain" (intransitive) down yesterday.

8. Correct as is. Unlike 7 above, a peahen may be "laying" (eggs), which a peacock (male) cannot do, thus: "I couldn't lie down where the peahen had laid (eggs) yesterday."

Avoiding Repetition

The repetition of words in English composition is a major stylistic error. Consider the following abominable passage:

> *To complete the sculpture, Baby Bear needed a candelabrum, a spatula, and three leaky bicycle inner tubes which needed to be inflated repeatedly almost to the bursting point and needed to be covered with birdseed and vermiculite.*

Note the repetition of the word *needed*. Using the word once is acceptable, twice is revolting, and three times, unforgivable.

There are a number of ways to repair word repetitions in a passage. One may simply replace instances of the offending term with synonyms, or rework the material to avoid the problem altogether. (Note that this sentence could have been *"There are a number of ways to repair word repetitions in a passage. One may simply replace instances of the offending word with synonyms, or rework the passage to avoid the problem altogether."* But the awkward multiple use of "word" and "passage" would have been repetitively repetitious.)

One improvement on our original sentence might be to use coordination:

> *To complete the sculpture, Baby Bear needed a candelabrum, a spatula, and three leaky bicycle inner tubes, which would require repeated inflation almost to the bursting point and a covering of birdseed and vermiculite.*

And another approach:

> *To complete the sculpture, Baby Bear needed a candelabrum, a spatula, and three leaky bicycle inner tubes, which were to be inflated repeatedly almost to the bursting point, and then covered with birdseed and vermiculite.*

Projects

1. Rewrite *Baby Bear and the Big Cheese* with synonyms.

2. Describe your own most bizarre experience with cheese.

3. Choose a position for or against the unrestricted use of non-traditional media in sculpture. Are there any media whose use should be illegal? Is there any subject matter that should be prohibited?

4. What sculpting medium would you choose to render your parents in?

Chapter 5

Vocabulary: The Billy Goats Gruff, the Sequel

Having determined that the troll did not in fact eat Billy goats, that it was a strict **herbivore**, and that its **reclusive misanthropic** behavior was due to a very painful ingrown toenail (or "toec-law" – it was hard to categorize) the **antagonists** set aside their **rancor** and came to an **amicable** agreement, which, in turn, developed into **reconciliation** and **benevolent camaraderie** as the four discussed politics, religion, and the relative **integrity** of straw, sticks, bricks, and gingerbread as construction material. The picnic lasted well into the afternoon as the three Billy goats grazed happily on the sweet grass on the other side of the bridge, while Eustace, for that was the troll's name, not **gregarious** by nature, was uncharacteristically sociable, set aside his customary **abstinence** for the **nonce**, and partook of gingerbread, icing, Skittles®, M&Ms®, and various other **anachronistic confections** salvaged from the foundation of a strangely **ornate** little house that middle Billy goat gruff had recently dis-

herbivore n. eater of vegetation

reclusive adj. solitary, unsociable

misanthropic adj. antisocial

antagonist n. adversary

rancor n. resentment

amicable adj. friendly

reconciliation n. agreement

benevolent adj. friendly

camaraderie n. comradeship

integrity n. soundness

gregarious adj. preferring company

abstinence n. act of refraining from

nonce n. time being

anachronistic adj. out-of-place in time

confection n. a sweet or candy

ornate adj. extensively ornamented

covered **inexplicably** abandoned in a nearby wood.

| | inexplicable adj. unexplainable |

"Much tastier than drywall." He mumbled between mouthfuls.

"No doubt" replied the **precocious** littlest Billy goat gruff "and certainly much more **aesthetic** when used in living and dining rooms than plaster or particle board, but its structural **integrity** is somewhat **evanescent**, especially when moist, and it's quite **deleterious** to the teeth."

precocious adj. talented

aesthetic adj. artistic

integrity n. soundness
evanescent adj. temporary
deleterious adj. harmful

"Most wall board is hard on the teeth", responded Eustace "and I do speak from experience."

"Ah, here he comes", announced the largest Billy goat gruff as a **venerable** cat in enormous **wellies** crossed the bridge carrying a black medical bag. "Our friend here is experiencing some discomfort."

venerable adj. respected
wellies n. overshoes

Sodbury (for so the cat called himself) was somewhat **wary** upon meeting the troll but, after some initial and quite understandable **trepidation**, he scrutinized the offending **digit** with **diligence**. A quick snip and a bandage put the **appendage** to rights again. Eustace was told to stay off the foot for a few hours, a highly **abbreviated** recovery period due to the extraordinary **resilience** of trolls.

wary adj. concerned

trepidation n. apprehension
digit n. finger or toe
diligence n. industriousness
appendage n. limb

abbreviated n. shortened
resilience n. ability to recover

"I wish they were all that easy", sighed Sodbury. "That lass in the glass coffin is a real puzzler. A real 'prince's kiss' case I think." The Billy goats and Eustace listened **raptly** to the **anecdote** as the cat recounted his experience with the seven odd little men and his inability to solve that case.

raptly adj. attentively
anecdote n. story

The littlest Billy goat suggested that if her recovery was **contingent** upon a

contingent adj. dependent

prince's kiss, he might know where one could be found to test the **hypothesis**.

hypothesis n. theory

"It mightn't be easy to persuade some **haughty** royal personage to leave the **opulence** of his castle and **condescend** to trek about the forest to kiss an unconscious maiden", responded the cat.

haughty adj. arrogant
opulence n. luxury
condescend v. stoop

"Oh, I don't think so", rejoined the littlest Billy goat. "Princes are a pretty dim lot and are generally ready to do the oddest things at the drop of a hat. Can't help thinking of one **intrepid** prince who based his romantic decisions entirely on shoe size."

intrepid adj. fearless

Eustace and the three goats agreed to collaborate with the cat in finding someone to wake the boxed beauty.

Glossary

abbreviate v. Shorten, abridge, reduce, truncate, curtail. Abbreviated adj. Abbreviation n.

abstinence n. Act of refraining from. Abstain [from] v. Abstemious adj.

appendage n. Limb, addition, attachment, adjunct, member, accessory.

aesthetic adj. Pertaining to beauty; artistic. Aesthetic n.

amicable adj. Agreeable; friendly, good-natured, harmonious. Amicability n.

anachronistic adj. Out-of-place in time. Anachronism n.

anecdote n. Short account of event; story, tale, yarn.
Anecdotal adj.

antagonist n. Opponent, adversary. Antagonistic adj.

benevolent adj. Friendly, helpful, kind, caring, benign.
Benevolence n.

camaraderie n. Trust among friends; amity, solidarity, comradeship.

collaborate v. To work together; join forces. Collaborative adj.
Collaboration n.

condescend [to] v. To descend to the level of another; stoop, deign, patronize. Condescension n.

condescending adj. Patronizing, disdainful, haughty, arrogant.

congregation n. An assembly of persons or things; collection, company, group, assemblage, crowd, host. Congregate v.

confection n. A sweet preparation such as candy.

contingent [upon, on] adj. Dependent upon events or outcomes not yet determined; dependent [upon, on], conditional, subject [to], reliant [on, upon].

deleterious [to] adj. Harmful, destructive, inimical, detrimental.

diligent adj. Hard-working; industrious, assiduous, meticulous, conscientious. Diligence n.

evanescent adj. Short-lived; transient, impermanent, ephemeral.

gregarious adj. Not habitually solitary or living alone; social, sociable, outgoing.

haughty adj. Arrogant, condescending, proud, conceited, snooty, self-important.

herbivore n. One that lives on vegetation. Herbivorous adj.

hypothesis n. Theory requiring proof; supposition, proposition, assumption. Hypothesize v. Hypothetical adj.

integrity n. Honesty, decency, the state of being unimpaired; soundness.

intrepid adj. Fearless, adventurous, brave, courageous.
Intrepidity n.

misanthropic adj. Characterized by hatred of humans; unfriendly, antisocial, hostile, malevolent. Misanthrope n.

nonce n. Present, time being.

opulent adj. Wealthy; lavish, luxurious, magnificent, sumptuous, affluent. Opulence n.

ornate adj. Elaborately, extensively ornamented; complex, highly wrought, complicated, flamboyant.

precocious adj. Talented beyond one's age; gifted, intelligent, talented. Precocity n.

rancorous adj. Hateful, resentful, ruthless, vengeful, fractious. Rancor n.

raptly adv. Attentively.

reclusive adj. Withdrawn, hermit-like; solitary, unsociable, secluded. Recluse n.

reconciliation [with] n. Agreement after a quarrel. Reconcile v.

resilience n. The ability to recover quickly; pliability flexibility toughness spirit. Resilient adj.

resilient adj. Quick to recover; flexible, tough, durable. Resilience n.

scrutinize v. To observe carefully;   inspect, examine, analyze. Scrutiny n.

trepidation n. Anxiety, fear, apprehension, consternation, foreboding.

venerable adj. Respectable due to age; respected, revered, honored, admired. Venerate v.

wary (of) adj. Watchful, alert, reticent, concerned, troubled.

Quiz

1. Eustace
   A. ate Billy goats.
   B. ate vegetation.
   C. preferred to eat drywall.
   D. suffered from scurvy.

2. Gingerbread
    A. was thought to lack integrity as construction material when moist.
    B. was less aesthetic than particleboard.
    C. was harder on the teeth than drywall.
    D. was an anachronistic confection.

3. Skittles®
    A. rained from the sky.
    B. were hard on the teeth.
    C. were very aesthetic with drywall.
    D. seemed out of place in time.

4. Sodbury
    A. was hard on the teeth.
    B. was a venerable cat.
    C. was a herbivore.
    D. looked ludicrous in gaudy socks.

5. Sodbury
    A. repaired the Billy goat's limb.
    B. tried to find a prince.
    C. was nervous when meeting Eustace.
    D. ate drywall.

6. Littlest Billy goat gruff
    A. was a haughty royal personage.
    B. was nervous when meeting Eustace.
    C. ate anachronistic confections.
    D. thought he might be able to find a prince.

7. The cat
    A. thought that persuading a prince to eat drywall was silly.
    B. knew where to find a prince.
    C. doubted that a prince would cooperate.
    D. based romantic decisions on shoe size.

8. The prince
    A. was needed to confirm a theory.
    B. wore enormous wellies.
    C. did not want to leave his castle.
    D. based romantic decisions on shoe size.

9. The Billy goats
    A. listened to the story of the maiden in the glass coffin.
    B. wore enormous wellies.
    C. did not eat trolls.
    D. ate Skittles® and M&Ms®.

10. Trolls
    A. eat Billy goats.
    B. eat vegetation.
    C. prefer to eat drywall.
    D. recover quickly.

11. Littlest Billy goat gruff
    A. was talented for his age.
    B. found an ornate little house.
    C. theorized that a prince's kiss was needed.
    D. suffered from scurvy.

Answers:

1. B	7. C
2. A	8. A
3. D	9. A
4. B	10. D
5. C	11. A
6. D	

Language Notes

Common Errors: Sentence Fragments

A sentence fragment is an incomplete structure that cannot stand on its own as a sentence:

- *When the Elephant hiccoughed.*
- *Using three pairs of slippery thermal underwear.*
- *To invoke the spirit of the compost pile.*
- *In a desperate effort to avoid familial distractions.*
- *Or else the cat might roll in the butter all afternoon.*

Avoid using fragments like these as sentences. However, these dependent clauses are very useful in building sentences, to add information to a complete thought. For example: *When the Elephant hiccoughed he blew a chartreuse bubble out his trunk.*

Common Errors: the Run-on Sentence

Run-on sentences are independent sentences either linked with a comma (the comma splice), or simply run end to end (the fused sentence) and are regarded as improper:

> *Telephone tag has become a serious health hazard, it is particularly dangerous in a crowded office or with older heavier equipment.*

> *Lawn mowers don't run well on catsup some varieties are highly corrosive.*

Run-ons are easily corrected by creating two separate sentences, making one a dependent clause, or by linking the phrases with a semicolon, or a conjunction.

Telephone tag has become a serious health hazard, particularly in a crowded office or with older, heavier equipment.

Telephone tag has become a serious health hazard; it is particularly dangerous in a crowded office or with older, heavier equipment.

Telephone tag has become a serious health hazard and is particularly dangerous in a crowded office or with older, heavier equipment.

Lawn mowers don't run well on catsup; some varieties are highly corrosive.

Lawn mowers don't run well on catsup as some varieties are highly corrosive.

Varied Sentence Structure

Writing that does not venture beyond very basic sentence structure creates the impression of an author with very poor language skills. Consider the first paragraph of the story:

Having determined that the troll did not in fact eat Billy goats, that it was a strict herbivore, and that its reclusive misanthropic behavior was due to a very painful ingrown toenail, the antagonists set aside their rancor and came to an amicable agreement, which, in turn, developed into reconciliation and benevolent camaraderie as the four discussed politics, religion, and the relative integrity of straw, sticks, bricks, and gingerbread as construction material.

This would probably have been written quite differently by a student in the third or fourth grade. Even with sophisticated vocabulary, it would sound very primitive if it read like this:

The antagonists determined that the troll did not eat Billy goats. They learnt that it was a strict herbivore. They found that its behavior was due to an ingrown toenail. They set aside their rancor. They came to an amicable agreement. This became a reconciliation and benevolent camaraderie. Then the four discussed politics and religion. They talked about sticks. They talked about bricks. They discussed the relative integrity of straw, sticks, bricks, and gingerbread as construction material.

The complex first sentence of this story could have been written using these ten simple sentences instead, but would then sound like the work of a ten year old, despite the vocabulary.

The Dependent Clause

While a sentence must have one and only one independent clause, it may have any number of dependent clauses, though it should not contain so many that it becomes difficult to understand.

Examples of dependent clauses:

1. Having determined that the troll did not in fact eat Billy goats
2. that it was a strict herbivore
3. that its reclusive misanthropic behavior was due to a very painful ingrown toenail
4. which, in turn, developed into reconciliation
5. as the four discussed politics

Clauses that start with subordinating elements including *that, which, as, because, since, else, before, whose, amid,* etc., are sentence fragments, and, though a dependent clause on its own is a fragment, they can help to add interest and variety to writing.

Examine the use of subordinate clauses in the reading passage.

Combining Sentences

Combine the following groups of sentences into single sentences with multiple clauses.

For example:

1. The mastodon was furious.

2. The mastodon's bicycle had been buried in the compost pile.

    Combined sentence: The mastodon, whose bicycle had been buried in the compost pile, was furious.

1. The pleasantly argumentative tour guide avoided the flock of confused ducks.

2. The ducks were trying to pick the coffee beans out of the coal scuttle.

1. Rupert plied the recalcitrant postman with questions.

2. Most of the questions dealt with dark energy in the expanding universe.

1. The starboard nacelle had been infested with tribbles.

2.   The fluffy coats of the tribbles could be knitted into excellent bicycle seats.

1. The function returned a strange value.

2. The value appeared to be unrelated to the parameters passed.

3. The value was, however, a function of parameters passed in the subsequent three calls to the function.

1. The chef was unable to wrest the spatula from the unintelligible Mancunian.

2. The Mancunian's Dachshund bore a rhinestone howdah on its back.

3. The howdah was occupied by two inimical chipmunks.

Projects

1. Construct five sentences each containing at least three anachronisms. Use dependent clauses extensively; experimenting with how many can be included without obscuring the meaning and readability of the sentence. (For example: *The centurion ruthlessly gobbled up all the green Skittles before stepping into the transporter amid thunderous applause from the Cossacks whose gaudy socks clashed dreadfully with their fur lined skateboards and intricately embroidered sneakers depicting mammoth and mastodon migrations.*)

2. Describe any construction project involving confections. Use extravagant dependant clauses, imagination, and gobs of icing.

3. Formulate and describe a hypothesis that can be disproved using a handsaw and/or a squeegee.

Chapter 6

Vocabulary: The Jurassic Cavalcade

After Uncle Cuthbert's office of Institutional Direction and Credentialing (IDC) had become almost universally referred to as the office of Idiocy Damage Control, its name was officially changed to the office of **Matriculation** and Educational Advancement (MEA). Later that same week at a meeting of the academic senate in which Uncle Cuthbert, in a move of unprecedented **fatuity**, had presented a program for improving **remedial** English scores by omitting those test questions from previous semesters which had brought down the average, professor Finnek was inspired to refer to the newly dubbed MEA as the Ministry of **Erroneous** Assumptions. The **aptness** of the **appellation** was **irrefragable** and Uncle Cuthbert sensed instantly that this **epithet** would henceforth ineluctably adhere to his office. Indeed, within days all recollection of the official designation for the MEA was forgotten and supplanted with the new **sobriquet**.

After a raucous parade including a choir of **didgeridoos** and a stilt-

matriculation n. admission

fatuity n. foolishness
remedial adj. corrective

erroneous adj. mistaken
apt adj. suitable
appellation n. name
irrefragable adj. undeniable
epithet n. nickname

sobriquet n. epithet

didgeridoo n. Australian musical instrument

walking panda, which had students, faculty and staff flocking from classrooms and all corners of the campus, the Society for Conscientious Deferential Irreverence mounted a skit in which **canonical** assumptions in chemistry, music and anthropology were redefined in accordance with freshmen exam results from the previous semester, resulting in toxic diet sodas, **cacophonous** commercial jingles and the discovery of a tribe of **caribou** herding **Masai** in northern Finland.

canonical adj. generally accepted

cacophonous adj. discordant

caribou n. reindeer

Masai proper noun East African Tribe

Little was heard from the MEA for many months. The **ignominy** into which that office had sunk as an indirect result of Boadicea's comedic **thespian diatribe** had made her Uncle Cuthbert extremely wary of following the time-honored tradition of frivolous and pointless **pettifoggery** lest he and other members of the administration be similarly subjected to **demeaning** public ridicule.

ignominy n. disgrace

thespian adj. stage related
diatribe critique

pettifoggery n. deceptive speech
demeaning adj. humiliating

Uncle Cuthbert had dealt with **disparagement** very effectively in the past, largely by **equivocation** and **obfuscation** but Boadicea and her growing cabal of cohorts were eagerly anticipating any effort to obscure and mislead and it seemed that he might be forced to produce something **unassailable** and of lasting value. However, the spirit of college administration was far too strong in Uncle Cuthbert who

disparagement n. ridicule

equivocation n. misleading speech
obfuscation n. confusion

unassailable adj. irrefutable

instead took the route of inaction, as that would, if used in moderation, provide little fuel for parody, and if prolonged, might outlast the **fervor** generated by her previous production - ploys clearly preferable to having to **fabricate** anything valid.

fervor n. zeal

fabricate v. manufacture

Far from diminishing, the **ardor** of her **rebarbative cadre** increased through some minor **interstitial** successes including a water ballet in protest of the College's decision to enter into an exclusive agreement with a soft drink corporation for the installation of vending machines to dispense exorbitantly expensive toxin-laden stimulants.

ardor n. passion
rebarbative adj. annoying
cadre n. core of revolutionaries
interstitial adj. in-between

Forced into action, a half-hearted attempt at **placating** detractors was made but it failed miserably to evade an **opprobrious** onslaught. A pageant of **squamous Brobdingnagian papier-mâché colossi** was designed, conceived, constructed and paraded - each reptilian **visage** bearing an unmistakable likeness to a member of the administration, including one very baffled looking **diplodocus** (indisputably Uncle Cuthbert) - through the campus and up the avenue. Boadicea, acutely aware of, and reveling in, the **anachronism** (millions of years before the appearance of **eohippus**), dubbed it a **Jurassic cavalcade.**

placate v. pacify

opprobrious adj. disdainful
squamous adj. scaly
Brobdingnagian adj. huge
papier-mache n. construction material
visage n. face

diplodocus n. dinosaur
anachronism n. temporal anomaly
eohippus n. early horse
Jurassic n. geologic period of the dinosaurs
cavalcade n. procession of horses

Glossary

agoraphobia n. Fear of open spaces. Agoraphobic adj.

anachronism n. An instance of someone existing or an event occurring in other than proper chronological, historical sequence. A time anomaly.

appellation n. Name, title, designation. Term, address, cognomen,
moniker, nickname, description, epithet, sobriquet.

apt adj. Precisely suitable, appropriate, fitting, felicitous.

ardor n. Fiery intensity, passion, zeal, avidity, sedulity.

Brobdingnagian adj. Immense, enormous, gigantic, huge, vast.

cacophonous. adj. Discordant, dissonant, having a harsh, unpleasant, jarring sound. Cacophony n.

cadre n. A core of competent individuals around whom a larger
(often revolutionary) body can form.

cavalcade n. A procession of horses.

canonical. adj. Conforming to orthodox or widely-accepted regulations or guidelines.

caribou n. A reindeer.

demeaning adj. Belittling, humiliating, degrading, debasing, derogatory. Demean v.

diatribe n. A bitter, excoriating denunciation. Tirade, abuse, criticism, reviling, harangue, invective, vituperation, pejorative.

didgeridoo or didjeridu n. A musical instrument of the Australian
Aborigines consisting of a long hollow tree limb or bamboo stalk that makes a deep drone when blown into.

diplodocus n. A large herbivorous Jurassic-Epoch dinosaur of the
Sauropod suborder.

disparagement n. A show of disrespect, contempt, criticism, ridicule, condemnation, scorn, depreciation, disdain, denunciation, derision, denigration, derogation. Disparage v.

eohippus n. Hyracotherium. The earliest known horse species
which lived about 50 million years ago during the early
Eocene Epoch (Long after the Jurassic period).

epithet n. A (commonly deprecatory) term used to characterize a person or thing. A label, name, title, description, tag, nickname, designation, appellation, sobriquet, moniker. Epithetic adj.

equivocation n. A statement open to multiple interpretations and often intended to mislead. Ambiguity, casuistry, sophistry, chicanery, speciousness, sophism. Equivocate v. Equivocal adj.

erroneous adj. In error, false, mistaken. incorrect, wrong, flawed, fallacious, faulty, inaccurate, untrue, invalid, unfounded, spurious, amiss, unsound.

fabricate v. To make, build or construct. Manufacture, form, fashion, shape, frame, assemble, erect.

fatuity n. Foolishness, stupidity, absurdity, folly. Fatuous adj.

fervor n. Hot, intense emotion. Arousal, excitement, zeal, enthusiasm, ardor, passion. Fervid adj.

gustatory adj. Of or relating to the sense of taste.

ignominy n. Opprobrium, disgrace, disrepute, dishonor, humiliation, shame. Ignominious adj.

interstitial adj. Occupying the space in between other things, objects or events. Interstice n. A small opening between things.

irrefragable adj. Impossible to refute or controvert, incontrovertible, indisputable, undeniable, irrefutable. Irrefragability n.

Jurassic adj. Of or relating to the geologic period from about 208 to 144 million years ago.

Masai or Maasai Proper noun. An East-African people of Kenya and Tanzania.

matriculation n. The process of being admitted into a group, especially a college or university. Admission, admittance. Matriculate v.

obfuscation n. The act of rendering something confusing and incomprehensible. Evasiveness, deception, equivocation, prevarication, sophistry, obliqueness, sophism.

opprobrious adj. Expressing contemptuous disdain or reproach. Scornful, abusive, belittling, disdainful, contemptuous, disparaging. Opprobrium. n.

panacea n. A remedy or medicine proposed for or professing to cure all diseases; cure-all, solution.

papier-mâché n. A combination of paper pulp and glue which can be sculpted or molded.

pettifoggery n. The act of quibbling over details and definitions, often for purposes of diversion and deception.

placate v. To appease or pacify, assuage, conciliate, lenify, mollify, calm, tranquilize.

rebarbative adj. Irritating, repellent, annoying, harassing, harrying.

remedial adj. Healing or providing remedy. Treating or overcoming deficiencies. Therapeutic, salubrious, healing, curing, curative, health-promoting, alleviative, salutary, corrective.

sobriquet n. An affectionate or humorous nickname or assumed name. Appellation, appellative, designation, denomination.

squamous adj. Scaly. Squamulose.

thespian adj. Relating to drama and the stage.
n. An actor.

unassailable adj. Impossible to dispute or disprove. Indisputable, irrefragable, incontrovertible, undeniable, irrefutable, proven, positive, absolute, conclusive, incontestable.

visage n. Face, lineament, appearance, likeness, countenance, aspect.

Quiz

1. The program Uncle Cuthbert presented
    A. was laden with canonical assumptions
    B. involved a stilt-walking Panda.
    C. was inane.
    D. was renamed.

2. Professor Finnek
   A. presented a program for improving test scores.
   B. played the didgeridoo.
   C. coined a new sobriquet for the MEA.
   D. preferred the original name for the IDC.

3. The SCDI
   A. produced a skit about a panda.
   B. drew attention to their skit with didgeridoos.
   C. invented a new name for the MEA.
   D. discovered a tribe of caribou-herding Masai.

4. Masai tribesmen
   A. played the didgeridoo.
   B. were depicted as herding caribou.
   C. had sunk into ignominy.
   D. mounted a thespian diatribe.

5. In response to criticism,
   A. Uncle Cuthbert did nothing.
   B. Uncle Cuthbert produced something unassailable.
   C. Uncle Cuthbert entered into an agreement with a soft drink manufacturer.
   D. Uncle Cuthbert dressed up as a diplodocus.

6. The diplodocus
   A. was herded by Masai tribesmen.
   B. looked like uncle Cuthbert.
   C. presented a program to the academic senate.
   D. equivocated and obfuscated.

7. The rebarbative cadre
   A. put on a water ballet.
   B. attempted to placate detractors.
   C. word gaudy socks.
   D. herded caribou.

8. The Jurassic cavalcade
   A. made fun of Finnish Masai tribesmen.
   B. contained a diplodocus.
   C. was used to protest an exclusive soft-drink contract.
   D. took the route of inaction.

Answers

1. C.	5. A.
2. C.	6. B.
3. B.	7. A.
4. B.	8. B.

Language Notes

Count Nouns and Non-Countable (Mass) Nouns

In English, nouns that can be counted (count nouns) and those that cannot be counted (mass nouns) are handled very differently. In many cases count nouns and mass nouns are easily distinguished my simply asking whether making the noun plural and putting "how many", a definite article, or a number in front of it makes more sense than putting "how much" in front:

Count nouns:

- A pencil: three pencils

- A frog: three frogs

- A minister: three ministers.

Mass nouns are uncomfortable with numbers:

- A confusion: three confusions (No. "How much confusion")

- An air: three airs (No, "How much air")

- A misery: three miseries (No, "How much misery")

- A research: three researches (No, "How much research")

Many nouns can be both count and mass nouns, often with different meanings.

Paper:

- How much paper? (24 reams, boxes, rolls of paper)

- How many papers? (He published three papers on invertebrate alcoholism last year)

Oil:

- How much oil? (one quart)

- How many oils? (olive oil, corn oil, linseed oil — three oils.)

Mystery:

- Much mystery surrounds the case of the giant rat of Sumatra.

- There are probably many more mysteries set in English country houses than murders in all of Yorkshire.

Thought:

- Not much thought has been given to making cats amphibious.

- Did Rupert have any thoughts about wearing gaudy socks in the parade?

The Web Searching Solution

When in doubt about the countability of a noun, one could just compare the result count from a search for "much [noun]" to that from a search for "many [noun]s". The search, "many confusions" yielded 55,900, while "much confusion" produced 774,000. While searching "how much" with most countable nouns will reveal clearly that the noun does not function as a mass noun ("how much pencil", "how much bicycle", "how much flagpole"), this process is not always reliable because, as demonstrated above, some nouns can be both countable and non-countable. The respective counts of "many thoughts" and "much thought" do not differ greatly. In these cases, a targeted search and an examination of context is probably best.

Frequently the excerpts Google presents are perfectly adequate for understanding usage and there is no need to visit the pages found as demonstrated in the following excerpts from the first page of results of a search restricted to academic sites in the UK.

Searched: site:ac.uk/ "many thoughts are"

> Within a given conceptual space, *many thoughts are* possible, only some of which may have been actually thought.

> As *many thoughts are* in my mind: As wavelets o'er thee roam;: As many wounds are in my heart: As thou hast flakes of foam. But if heaven's constellations

> One problem of this work is that too *many thoughts are* embedded in a single character-mind. It is often difficult to identify to whom each thought...

Searched: site:ac.uk/ "much thought is"

> ... *much thought is* already being given to the social and economic implications of these changes.

> *Much thought is* given to the dating and composition of Weissenburg's cartulary, which is put in the context of Louis the German's attempts to acquire...

> ... But modern versions of RTM assume that *much thought is* not grounded in mental images. The classic contemporary treatment maintains, instead, ...

The resultant phrases reveal clearly how the word is used in context.

Remember, mass nouns do not take indefinite articles and are quantified by:

> "how much [noun]" or "how little [noun]" and "more [noun]", "less [noun], all that [noun] or the amount of [noun]"

while countable nouns use:

> "how many [noun]s" or "how few [noun]s", "more [noun]s", "fewer [noun]s" or the quantity of [noun]s.

Note that the comparative form "more" is used with both countable and non-countable nouns. Purists maintain that "fewer" should always be the comparative form used with countable nouns but the use of "less" in these contexts is increasing: "Oatmeal has less calories than granola". When searched, the count was: "less calories", 491,000 and "fewer calories", 6,060,000. It will be interesting to see how these numbers change over time.

There are some sticky areas however. Some count nouns, when used in plural, and particularly when large quantities are discussed, tend to be treated as mass nouns. Phrases such as "the amount of lentils" (460,000,000) tend to compete well with the more correct "the quantity of lentils" (475,000,000).   With more abstract nouns, this is even more evident.

"quantity of resources" 463,000

"number of resources" 8,770,000

"amount of resources" 11,500,000

Some Mass Nouns

(Be sure to look up any you don't know)

A few mass nouns:

acrimony	celerity	graffiti
adulation	cheese	grass
advice	cloth	hair
air	dancing	harm
aluminum	disdain	heat
applause	dust	history
apostasy	economics	hockey
approbation	electricity	homework
avarice	equipment	housework
badinage	experience	ice
beer	fatuity	information
biology	fealty	insouciance
blood	flour	knowledge
boating	flummery	leather
cacography	food	logorrhea
cake	furniture	luggage
casuistry	glass	mathematics

meat	publicity	software
mentation	rancor	subservience
metal	reading	steel
milk	research	sugar
money	reticence	sunshine
militancy	revulsion	temerity
music	rice	traffic
oxygen	rodomontade	transportation
photography	rubbish	travel
plastic	sand	water
poetry	sedulity	weather
pollution	smoking	wine
porcelain	soap	wood
probity	soccer	wool

Count and Mass Noun Usage

Mass nouns can usually be made countable by adding a count noun:

mass noun	count noun
furniture	piece of furniture
paper	sheet of paper
research	research paper

The use of count nouns as mass nouns can be intended for comic effect through the incongruity of the usage:

- It's 49 feet tall; how much flagpole do we really need?

- A tandem? What's he doing with that much bicycle?

If one prefers to avoid this effect, reference to size or quantity solves the problem: How large a flagpole? How big a bicycle? How long a piece of construction grade gingerbread?

Count Nouns and Mass Nouns Playsheet

Circle and fix the errors.

1. When dealing with a furniture of this size, Rupert had to agree that the word "mañana" conveyed far too acute a sense of urgency.

2. There was too much barrel of fermented applesauce for Hermione to deal with but less golf balls than the minimum required for the sleepover.

3. It wasn't me whom the assistant vice principal accused of impertinence after he saw so much of his bulletins, printed in the local newspaper with appropriate grammar corrections.

4. Rupert saw the curate and me mixing all that anchovy into the nougat.

5. Who do you think is responsible for putting so much toads into the library garden?

6. Whom should we make clean up all those peanut shells, tapioca, and horse droppings in the cafeteria after the Polo Club's cavalcade of ethnic indigenous cuisines?

7. There's too much reason for not letting Mrs. Drookle's second grade class reenact the Boston Tea Party at the Main Street fountain.

8. There's too much puce finger paint and Brillo pads to hide convincingly behind the irregularly eructative model volcano.

9. There's not enough volcano to hide even a small equipment.

10. Acrimonies abound in the field. Invertebrate alcoholisms seem to inspire many rancors.

Answers

1. Problem: "Furniture" is a mass noun. Search "much furniture" and "many furnitures" for the count. Correction: "When dealing with a piece of furniture of this size ..."

2. Problem: barrel is a count noun. Search "much barrel" and "many barrels".   Correction: "the barrel contained too much fermented applesauce ..." Problem: Golf ball is a count noun and "less" should be used only with mass nouns. It should be replaced with "fewer".

3. Problem: "bulletin" is a count noun. Search "much bulletin" and "many bulletins" for the count. Correction: "so many of his bulletins".

4. Problem: "anchovy" is a count noun. Search "much anchovy" and "many anchovies". Correction: "mixing all those anchovies" Note that the discrete fish can easily become a mass for culinary purposes and that usage may not be uncommon.

5. Problem: "toad" is a count noun. Search "much toads" many "toads". Correction: "So many toads".

6. Problem: "tapioca" is a mass noun listed with count nouns. Search "much tapioca" and "many tapiocas". Correction: "Whom should we make clean up all that tapioca and all those peanut shells, and horse droppings?

7. Problem: "reason" is, in this context, a count noun. Search "many reasons" and "much reason" . Correction: "There are too many reasons for…".

8. Problem: "Brillo pads" are countable. Search "much pad" and "many pads". Correction "There's too much puce finger paint and too many Brillo pads".

9. Problem: "volcano" is countable. Search "much volcano" and "many volcanoes". Problem: "equipment" is a mass noun: Search "much equipment" and "many equipments". Correction: "The volcano's not big enough to hide even a little equipment.

10. Problem: "acrimony", "alcoholism" and "rancor" are mass nouns. Search them. Correction: "Acrimony abounds in the field. Invertebrate alcoholism seems to inspire much rancor."

Projects

Rewrite *Stichwort College Weathers the Storm* in other words using the synonyms in the glossary for ideas.

Using words from the glossary:

1. Discuss the advantages and disadvantages of camera surveillance in public places. Who should have access to the files? Should people have the right to object to being photographed?

2. Do some research into the campus clubs and societies at colleges you are considering. Read their web pages, think about joining them and make a list of pros and cons.

3. What campus organizations would you want to see at a college that do not already exist. What events or projects would they sponsor?

Chapter 7

Vocabulary: The Prince

Littlest Billy goat led the **coterie** of co-conspirators to where he had seen the prince in question. A **conformist** and thus an **exemplary** instance of the **genre**, this prince was a **precocious orator**, an **intuitive** swordsman, and an **impetuous**, if somewhat clueless, lover. Indeed, there he was, wearing **raiment** of **ostentatious opulence**, and **nonchalantly** dismembering a daisy with a vacant **adulatory** expression on his face as the group **surreptitiously** took a **circuitous** route around the clearing wherein the prince was moping.

coterie n. circle of friends

conformist n. traditionalist
exemplary adj. typical
genre n. category
precocious adj. talented
orator n. speaker
intuitive n. natural
impetuous n. rash
raiment n. clothing
ostentatious adj. showy
opulence n. luxury
nonchalant adj. casual
adulatory adj. adoring
surreptitious adj. secret
circuitous adj. roundabout

"This does not bode well", muttered Eustace reading significance into the **hackneyed** ritual, "it looks as though he already has somebody who loves him or loves him not. In either case he appears to be spoken for."

hackneyed adj. overused

"Oh, I wouldn't take that too seriously. It's likely to be just a **transient** and **inconsequential** infatuation. They're **inevitable** at his age. He probably doesn't even know her name or met her in a dream or something. I'm sure he's got a lot of kisses left in him for

transient adj. fleeting
inconsequential adj. trivial
inevitable adj. unavoidable

random maidens in distress", assured little Billy goat gruff. As if to **substantiate** this **hypothesis**, the prince suddenly broke into a song to his **anonymous** love. Delighted to hear his theory **vindicated**, the **diminutive ungulate** let out an inadequately **restrained** exclamation of **jubilation**, upon which the prince ceased **vocalizing**, turned quickly, and surveyed his surroundings.

"Well, that was less than **prudent**" **censured** the middle Billy goat gruff with **tactless disdain**.

"At least it stopped that awful singing", put in the **querulous** Sodbury; but he had spoken too soon. The **tenacious** prince, seeing nothing, quickly renewed his **crooning**. "I really can't take much more of this", **bemoaned** the cat. "Do we approach him now or just put him in a sack and go? What do we say to him?"

The plans each received some support but, as nobody had any good ideas on what to say to him, and the cat was becoming increasingly **exasperated** by the love song, a **compromise** was struck. They simply stuffed him into the sack, vowing to talk to him later when they had a more persuasive argument prepared. Although he continued to sing for a while, it was muffled enough to be bearable.

substantiate v. confirm
hypothesis n. theory
anonymous adj. nameless
vindicate v. prove correct
diminutive adj. small
ungulate n. hoofed animal
restrained adj. controlled
jubilation n. joy
vocalize v. produce voice sounds

prudent adj. wise
censure v. criticize
tactless adj. impolite
disdain n. scorn

querulous adj. irritable

tenacious adj. stubborn
croon v. sing

bemoan v. regret

exasperate v. irritate
compromise n. agreement

As it turned out, they simply handed the sack over to two **dumbfounded** but **ecstatic** dwarves standing guard over the glass coffin. The **disoriented** prince performed his task admirably upon release. No discredit to the more conventional interpretation of this incident is intended, for a prince wandering the wilds on his charger in hopes of some **fortuitous** encounter with a young lady does make a much better story (however improbable) than one arriving **inexplicably** in a sack transported by a **motley congregation** of animals. It is also perfectly understandable that truth and legend should **diverge** somewhat regarding

dumbfound v. confuse
ecstatic adj. delighted
disorient v. confuse

fortuitous adj. accidental

inexplicable adj. unexplainable
motley adj. miscellaneous
congregation n. collection
diverge v. be different

the lady's first words upon waking, which, as she excused herself briefly after her months of immobility, were somewhat more **mundane** and practical than romantic.

mundane adj. commonplace

The group, encouraged by their success, resolved to seek further opportunities to practice **compassionate** creativity.

compassionate adj. sympathetic

Glossary

adulation n. High praise; adoration, worship, admiration.
        Adulate v. Adulatory adj.
anonymous adj. Nameless, unidentified, unknown. Anonymity n.
bemoan v. To express grief over; lament, bewail, regret, mourn.
censure v./n. To criticize harshly; reprimand, reproach, condemn,
        remonstrate.
circuitous adj. Indirect, roundabout, meandering, winding. Circuity n.
compassion n. Sympathy, mercy, empathy, concern, consideration. Compassionate adj.
compassionate adj. Sympathetic, empathetic, concerned, kindly.
        Compassion n.
compromise v./n. To settle differences; to cooperate, to concede.
        Compromising adj.
conformist n. Follower of customs; traditionalist.   Conform v.
        Conformity n.
congregation n. Crowd of people; flock, group. Congregate v.
coterie n. A small, often select, group of persons who meet frequently for a purpose; click, assemblage.
croon v./n. To hum or sing softly; chant, drone.

disdain v./n. To regard with scorn, derision, disparagement, contempt. Disdainful adj.

disorient v. To cause to be disoriented, confused. Disoriented adj.

disoriented adj. Confused, unsettled, bewildered, perplexed, baffled. Disorient v.

diverge [from] v. Differ [from], deviate [from], depart [from], disagree [with]. Divergent adj.

divergent adj. Variant, moving apart, differing, deviating, contrary. Diverge v.

dumbfound v. To cause astonishment and perplexity; astonish, amaze, astound, stagger, confound, confuse, baffle, bewilder, flummox.

ecstatic adj. Delighted, overjoyed, thrilled, elated, rapturous, euphoric. Ecstasy n.

exasperation n. Irritation, frustration, annoyance, vexation. Exasperate n. Exasperated adj.

exemplary adj. Outstanding, excellent, commendable, typical. Exemplify v.

fortuitous adj. Lucky, accidental, chance, unexpected. Fortuity n.

genre n. A category, kind, type, sort, variety, genus.

hackneyed adj. Overused, clichéd, trite, worn-out.

hypothesis n.   Theory, supposition, proposition, assumption. Hypothetical adj. Hypothesize v.

impetuous adj. Rash, impulsive, hasty, reckless. Impetuosity n.

inconsequential adj. Trivial, unimportant, insignificant, negligible. Inconsequentiality n.

inevitable adj.   Unavoidable, certain, foreseeable, ineluctable. Inevitability n.

intuitive adj. Instinctive, natural, untutored, innate, instinctive. Intuition n. Intuit v.

jubilation n. Joy, exultation, elation, euphoria, delight. Jubilant adj. Jubilate v.

motley adj. Consisting of an incongruous mixture of types or colors; assorted, miscellaneous, diverse, varied, dissimilar.

mundane adj. Ordinary, common, routine, everyday, commonplace. Mundanity n.

nonchalant adj. Calm, casual, offhand, relaxed. Nonchalance n.

opulence n. Wealth, lavishness, luxury, magnificence.
    Opulent adj.
orator n. Speaker, lecturer, narrator. Orate v. Oration n.
ostentatious adj. Displaying wealth; pretentious, showy, boastful, affected, grandiose, flamboyant. Ostentation n.
precocious adj. Talented beyond one's age; gifted, intelligent, talented. Precocity n.
prudent adj. Wise, careful, cautious, sensible, discreet, wise.
    Prudence n.
querulous adj. Irritable, cantankerous, difficult, petulant, irascible.
raiment n. Garb, clothing, costume.
restrained adj. Controlled, restricted, reserved, calm, undemonstrative. Restrain v.
substantiate v. To verify, confirm, validate, authenticate, prove.
    Substantiation n.
surreptitious adj. Clandestine, stealthy, furtive, secret, sneaky, covert.
tactful adj. Diplomatic, polite, discreet, considerate.
    Tact n. Tactless ant.
tactless adj. Opposite of tactful.
tenacious adj. Persistent, resolute, stubborn, obstinate. Tenacity n.
transient adj. Of limited duration; fleeting, brief, temporary, momentary, transitory, ephemeral. Transience n.
    n. One who stays for only a short time; transitory, fleeting.
ungulate n. Hoofed animal.
vindicate v. To clear from blame; support, prove correct.

Quiz

1. The Prince
    A. was dressed casually.
    B. was a gifted speaker.
    C. ate daisies.
    D. ate drywall.

2. The daisy
   A. was being used for divination.
   B. was delightfully hackneyed.
   C. was being used for construction.
   D. was opulent.

3. The conspirators
   A. skirted the clearing furtively.
   B. dismembered a daisy.
   C. found an anonymous prince.
   D. were delighted at the hypothesis.

4. Little Billy Goat Gruff's theory
   A. was about a daisy.
   B. was disproven by a hackneyed ritual.
   C. was fatuous.
   D. was proven by a song.

5. The princess
   A. excused herself briefly.
   B. sang to her anonymous love.
   C. had no name.
   D. ate drywall.

6. The prince was in love with
   A. a princess named daisy.
   B. a transient infatuation.
   C. someone nameless.
   D. a sleeping princess.

7. _____ gave cry of delight.
   A. The prince
   B. A dwarf
   C. The cat
   D. The littlest Billy goat gruff

8. When put into a sack, the prince
    A. stopped singing.
    B. let out a cry of jubilation.
    C. started vocalizing.
    D. continued singing.

9. _____ was irascible.
    A. The diminutive ungulate
    B. Eustace
    C. Sodbury
    D. The dwarf

10. The prince's singing
    A. annoyed the dwarf.
    B. became muffled and bearable.
    C. dumbfounded Sodbury.
    D. was disoriented.

Answers

1. B
2. A
3. A
4. D
5. A
6. C
7. D
8. D
9. C
10. B

Language Notes

Lists, Coordination and Parallelism

In conjunction with subordinate clauses, lists help to add variety and interest to sentence structure. When a number of subjects are associated with a single verb, a number of verbs with a single subject, or multiple objects with a single subject/verb pair or a single preposition, they may be listed as a group. This parallel construct is known as coordination and must consist of words, phrases or clauses that are grammatically equivalent.

Multiple subjects:
> *The Troll, cat, and Billy goats discussed construction material.*

Multiple verbs:
> *The Billy goats discussed, complained, and argued about the relative advantages of gingerbread and drywall.*

Multiple clauses:
> *The Billy goats ate grass, tolerated gingerbread, and ignored drywall.*

Multiple objects:
> *The Billy goats ate grass, gingerbread, drywall, and just about anything else they could find.*

Listed items must be parallel, that is, the individual listed items must each fit into the sentence in the same way. Always check the integrity of your parallel construct by testing the items in context one at a time:
> *The Billy goats ate grass.*
> *The Billy goats ate gingerbread.*
> *The Billy goats ate drywall.*
> *The Billy goats ate just about anything else they could find.*

The items in a list are separated by commas, with a coordinating conjunction, an *and* or *or,* before the last one.   Whether there should be a comma before the *and* (the Oxford comma) depends on where you go to school and how anal your teacher is.   It is less common than it used to be.

Importantly, all of the items in the list must be of the same type – the same part of speech or a grammatically parallel phrase.   This is not acceptable:

> *The Billy goats were interested in*
>> *crossing the bridge,*
>> *discussing philosophy*
>> *to eat gingerbread.*

When expanded, the problem becomes obvious:
> *The Billy goats were interested in crossing the bridge.*
> *The Billy goats were interested in discussing philosophy.*
> *The Billy goats <u>were interested in to eat gingerbread.</u>*

In some cases, there may be a list within a list, but when this happens, it is not feasible to return to the outer list.   For example, this is acceptable:

> *The exhibit contained*
>> *A railway carriage,*
>> *A blunderbuss and*
>> *A painting depicting*
>>> *Mammoths*
>>> *Sabretooth cats and*
>>> *A ground sloth.*

This is not acceptable:

> *The exhibit contained*
>> *A railway carriage,*
>> *A blunderbuss,*

A painting depicting
Mammoths,
Sabretooth cats,
A ground sloth and
A display of Soviet-era excavation equipment.

This is not acceptable because the painting did not depict the display of excavation equipment and even if it did, the meaning is unclear and ambiguous.

Spoken Language in the USA

Though Standard Edited English is, for all practical purposes, the same in America as it is anywhere else, American scholars seem to stray further from the written standard in their speech than does the rest of the academic world. Even highly educated professors in the US, noticeably more than their foreign counterparts, tend toward an informal and generally very sloppy form of English that would require a great deal of editing to become acceptable on any college paper. It seems that most British, German, French, Swedish, Danish scholars speak flavors of English that are much closer to acceptable edited prose. It's hard to know exactly why Americans are so slovenly in their speech, but this auditory environment certainly explains why American students have such difficulty mastering standard written English.

A case in point: In a DVD accompanying an Astronomy text, a number of eminent astronomers (who shall remain nameless) gave short presentations on and explanations of astronomical phenomena. In this video, SAT errors were committed frequently by the American astronomers, far more than by the Belgian, Danish or British scientists. That scholars in the US appear to put little effort into polishing their informal spoken language is very evident in these examples and its absence in a work that is presented as an example to students is particularly distressing.

Everyone makes mistakes in speaking. Elsewhere in the academic world however, it is not at all uncommon to hear a speaker straying briefly down an ungrammatical path, becoming aware of the problem and making an instantaneous correction. But in the US, speakers charge ruthlessly, unabashedly and remorselessly on, callously mangling and mutilating their spoken language with unconscionable, indiscriminate abandon and utterly without embarrassment or contrition.

For example: Redundancy is not acceptable in polished English. Sometimes this repetition is referred to as a pleonasm. This is particularly grating:

> *"...[we are] producing an ever increasingly more sophisticated model of the universe."*

These are acceptable:

> *An ever increasingly sophisticated model*

> *An ever more sophisticated model*

This type of error is to be avoided in written English and is hunted down and eliminated by any good editor.

Here is a mismatched parallelism example from the same DVD (in this case gerund/infinitive mismatch):

> *"...[they were] less interested in answering the scientific questions than to support the emperor's power."*

This problem can be best demonstrated by expanding the parallel constructs out:

> *They were interested in answering the scientific questions.*

> *They were <u>interested to support</u> the emperor's power.*

This second sentence clearly does not conform to any collocation standard.

Or, the worst case of all, a statement that simply does not say what the speaker means:

> *"... This stellar body emits two streams of energy on either side."*

Of course, what is meant is:

> *... This stellar body emits two streams of energy, one on either side.*

This demonstrates another critical aspect of good language. Well crafted language means what it is supposed to mean. Sloppy language is at best imprecise and frequently thoroughly misleading.

These are all classic SAT errors of the sort that are addressed on almost every exam. The butchery of language is even more common of course in spoken lectures in secondary school classrooms, but this kind of error seems to appear much less frequently in the speech of foreign academics and is rarely to be found in the language of British scholars. A more rigorous study would be interesting.

Parallelism Playsheet

Circle the errors in the following. Below each sentence, write your corrected version.

1. The cloth emu has several advantages: it isn't classified as luggage, you aren't required to check it at the door, to open it, the overall whimsical effect, and nobody will guess you have a saxophone.

2. When we heard the curate coming, Penelope hid the saxophone, Hermione, the liver pâté, and Boadicea, the greasy overalls; so that he would find it harder to guess what we had been up to.

3.   On the third floor you will find collector's editions, scuba
      equipment, tribal headgear, and a discount bin of assorted
      flanges, bushings, cams, and a display of second century
      Roman baldrics.

4.   Thus far only chewing gum, singing, certain violent card
      games, and to do Stephen's infamous Groucho Marx impres-
      sion were strictly forbidden, though after today, quoting Spi-
      noza is likely to be added to the list.

Answers

1.   The cloth emu has several advantages: it isn't classified as
      luggage, you aren't required to check it at the door, to open it,
      the overall whimsical effect, and nobody will guess you have
      a saxophone. **Unparallel:**

>   *the cloth emu has several advantages:*

>> *It isn't classified as luggage (sentence)*

>> *You aren't required to*

>>> *check it at the door (fragment, start of a sub list)*

>>> *To open it (fragment, continuation of the sub list)*

>> *Nobody will know you have a saxophone. (sentence re-
turning to the outer list)*

2.   When we heard the curate coming, Penelope hid the saxo-
      phone, Hermione, the liver pâté, and Boadicea, the greasy
      overalls; so that he would find it harder to guess what we
      had been up to. **No error.**

3.   On the third floor you will find collector's editions, scuba
      equipment, tribal headgear, and a discount bin of assorted

flanges, bushings, cams, and a display of second century Roman baldrics. **Unparallel**.

On the third floor you will find

   Collectors editions

   scuba equipment

   tribal headgear

   a discount bin of assorted

      flanges,

      bushings,

      cams

and a display of second century Roman baldrics.

Unless the display of second century Roman baldrics was in the discount bin, this is unparallel.

4. Thus far only chewing gum, singing, certain violent card games, and to do Stephen's infamous Groucho Marx impression were strictly forbidden, though after today, quoting Spinoza is likely to be added to the list. **Unparallel**:

   Thus far only

      chewing gum (Noun)

      singing (Noun)

      certain violent card games (Noun)

      and to do Stephen's Groucho Marx impression (infinitive verb phrase)

   were strictly forbidden.

The first three are nouns and thus parallel. The last one is an infinitive phrase "to do Stephen's Grouch Marx impression" and does not fit. Correction: "and doing Stephen's Groucho Marx impression". This solves the problem by making the infinitive into a gerund to fit with the other nouns.

Projects

1. Choose a commonly known tale and improve upon it using vocabulary from this and other chapters.

2. Devise, define, and describe three parlor games, annoying practical jokes, or decorative mobiles involving paper clips, drier lint, feathers, and/or linguini. Use lists, making sure all constructs are parallel.

Chapter 8

Vocabulary: Cinderella

The kingdom of Zweifel seemed to be suffering from a **dearth** of eligible maidens, at least those eligible to marry royalty. Refusing to **defer** to **ludicrous** ancient custom, Prince Unschuld proposed to remedy this **paucity** by **abrogating** those restrictive regulations and establishing new **criteria**. The **criterion** of noble birth having been **rescinded**, a great ball was announced and all **denizens** of the kingdom were invited.

dearth n. lack
defer v. yield
ludicrous adj. ridiculous
paucity n. lack
abrogate v. nullify by official decree
criteria n. plural of criterion
criterion n. standard of judgment
rescind v. abolish
denizen n. resident

Cinderella, an avid **bibliophile**, whose **torpid, bellicose** stepsisters constantly **derided** her, was resolved to attend over their objections. Seemingly **devoid** of hope, the **lachrymose** lady, moping in her **squalid** quarters, suddenly saw a very strange sight. It was unmistakably a troll, wearing a tiara, holding a magic wand, prancing about gracefully, and **proffering** garments of **vermilion, puce, azure,** and **chartreuse**. Unconvinced by his assurance that this was the current fashion, her enthusiasm for the opportunity was such that she accepted his offer of **garish garb** without **demur** and did not even question his claim to be her fairy

bibliophile n. book lover
torpid adj. lazy
bellicose adj. belligerent
deride v. ridicule
devoid (of) adj. lacking
lachrymose adj. tearful
squalid adj. dirty, neglected

proffer v. to present or offer
vermilion, puce, azure, chartreuse: colors

garish adj. tasteless, loud
garb n. clothing
demur n. to object

god troll. Arrayed in her new **reful-gent chromatic raiment**, she was transported to the ball in a **troika** pulled by three goats whose **feline** coachman was sporting enormous

refulgent adj. gleaming
chromatic adj. colorful
raiment n. costume
troika n. carriage drawn by three across
feline n./adj. belonging to the cat family

footwear. She attended the ball and spent the evening **regaling** the prince with **trivia** and **persiflage**.

regale v. entertain
trivia n. trifles
persiflage n. good natured talk

Cinderella's stepsisters were duly repaid for their **egregious** behavior and, as a **didactic** measure, were made to dwell in Cinderella's old quarters

egregious adj. conspicuously bad
didactic adj. instructive

which reeked of **toxic effluvium**. | toxic adj. poisonous
Cinderella wedded the prince and | effluvium n. yucky stuff
lived happily ever after. |

Glossary

abrogate v. To abolish, repeal, revoke, rescind, annul, retract.
    Abrogation n.
bellicose adj. Warlike, belligerent, pugnacious, combative, con-
    frontational. Bellicosity adj.
bibliophile n. One who loves books. Bibliophilic adj.
chromatic adj. Abounding in color; colorful. Chromaticism n.
criterion n.   A standard of judgment;   decisive factor, principle,
    measure, condition, reason. Plural: criteria
dearth n. Scarcity, paucity, lack, shortage, insufficiency,
    deficiency.
defer v. To yield out of respect or consideration of another's wish-
    es, age or authority; postpone, suspend. Deferrable adj.
demur n. Objection, protest.
    v. To object, protest, balk, doubt.
denizen n. Inhabitant, resident, citizen, native.
deprecate v. To belittle; to minimize; to undervalue,   disparage,
    denigrate, derogate, detract, decry.
    Deprecatory adj. Deprecation n.
depreciation n. A lowering in value or an underrating in worth.
deride v. To ridicule; scoff, disparage, disparage, disdain.
    Derision n. Derisive adj.
devoid (of) adj. Lacking, missing, wanting.
didactic adj. Intended for instruction; educational, instructive, edi-
    fying. Didacticism n.
effluvium n. A noxious or ill-smelling exhalation from decaying
    or putrefying matter. Effluvial adj.
egregious adj. Conspicuously bad or offensive.
garb n. Clothing, dress, attire, costume.
garish adj. Brash, bright, loud, dazzling, tasteless, gaudy.

gaudy adj. Garish, flashy, kitschy, extravagant, loud, colorful.

lachrymose adj. Tearful, crying, weepy, sobbing. Lachrymate v.
       Lachrymation n.

ludicrous adj. Ridiculous, absurd, preposterous, foolish, comical.

Paucity Scarcity, lack, shortage, insufficiency, deficiency,
       exiguity.

persiflage n. Light or frivolous chatter; banter, light teasing.

proffer v./n. To offer, present; hold out, extend, tender, submit.

refulgent adj. Shining radiantly; gleaming, glowing, luminous,
       radiant. Refulgence n.

regale v. Amuse, delight, divert, entertain. Regalement n.

rescind v. Abolish, withdraw, annul, cancel, repeal, overturn.
       Rescindable adj. Rescindment n.

squalid adj. Dirty and wretched; filthy, foul, nasty, fetid.
       Squalor n.

torpid adj. Sluggish, listless, lethargic, lazy, languorous, stagnant.
       Torpor n.

toxic adj. Poisonous; lethal, venomous. Toxin n.

trivia n. An assortment of inconsequential odds and ends; triviali-
       ties, trifles. Plural of trivium. Trivial adj.

troika n. Carriage drawn by three horses abreast.

Quiz

1. Cinderella was
    A. fond of pumpkins.
    B. fond of colors.
    C. fond of books.
    D. unable to go to the ball.
    E. fond of horses.

2. When Cinderella first saw her 'fairy god troll,' she was
    A. livid.   B. crying.
    C. dejected.   D. plotting sedition.
    E. phlegmatic.

3. Cinderella's 'fairy god troll' presented her with
    A. colorful clothing.   B. regal clothing.
    C. gaudy socks.   D. effluvium.
    E. books.

4. The kingdom of Zweifel suffered from
    A. toxic effluvium.
    B. bad taste.
    C. gaudy socks.
    D. a dearth of fairy godmothers.
    E. a paucity of marriageable girls.

5. Prince Unschuld favored _____ marriage regulations in the Kingdom of Zweifel.
    A. nullifying   B. suspending
    C. augmenting   D. reviving
    E. eroding

6. _____ were invited to the ball.
    A. All nubile females
    B. All marriageable maidens
    C. All inhabitants of the kingdom
    D. All stepsisters
    E. All eligible maidens

7. Cinderella's stepsisters had to live in Cinderella's old quarters _____
    A. to teach them a lesson.
    B. to punish them.
    C. and wear gaudy socks.
    D. and measure their feet.
    E. and make shoes.

8. Cinderella and the prince talked about _____
    A. trivialities.
    B. gaudy socks.
    C. toxic effluvium.
    D. matters of state.
    E. old quarters.

9. Cinderella attended the ball _____
    A. with her stepsisters.
    B. in glass slippers.
    C. in colorful clothes.
    D. reluctantly.
    E. for the first time.

10. Cinderella's room _____
    A. smelled bad.
    B. was in the basement.
    C. was colorful.
    D. was inappropriate for entertaining.
    E. was drab.

Answers

1. C.
2. B.
3. A.
4. E.
5. A.
6. C.
7. A.
8. A.
9. C.
10. A.

Language Notes

An Auditory Approach To English Language Skills Acquisition. Speaking Well Is The Key To Writing Well. How To Improve One's Feel For Language

While speaking well is indeed the key to writing well, it's not as easy as it sounds. How many people actually speak well and how often do students hear well-spoken English? Unfortunately English of the quality expected on the written papers of college applicants is rarely spoken or heard. Is it possible to expose children to language that will improve rather than damage their intrinsic language sense? Yes!

The static and silent tome has served scholars well for many centuries but has been failing for nearly as long to move and inspire language in students. Though there are certainly those, even among auditory learners, to whom the book does successfully convey knowledge and language, the child (even the literate reader) acquires much of his/her language art from speech, from hearing dialog, argument, songs, stories - and in the absence of aural input worthy of emulation, the road to facile literacy takes a decidedly uphill turn. It is nonetheless still possible, even without an exemplary parental role model, and despite public school, to find examples of diction that can ignite the spark of eloquence and serve learners well in their academic careers, but to achieve this, one is well advised to seek external input. Sources do abound though. No longer is the written word the only channel available for education.

The College Board, the body responsible for a number of standardized exams, including the SAT, has defined a set of grammar rules which it regards as essential to formal written English. Some of the rules in this list have been disputed (*See* Disputed Aspects of English Grammar p200), but in general, it is a solid set of grammar concepts and should definitely be studied by the would-be college student. Though these are essential language standards in academia, most commonly heard speech violates them consistently, as mangled idioms, colloquialisms, syntactic mismatches, dangling and misplaced modifiers, confused and inconsistent tenses, misused words and unparallel constructs pollute much non-academic (and even academic) informal English so thoroughly that reliable sources of language worthy of emulation can be very hard to find. How can today's student hope to sense or feel the right way to express an idea when perpetually subjected to a verbal inundation of ill-formed syntax?

When listening to teachers in class or school meetings televised on community access channels, one is struck by the banality of the language even when the grammar is not irredeemably awful. What hope does the student have whose ears have been so thoroughly steeped in communication contaminated with misusage and largely bereft of any spark of inspired expression? With nothing but flawed and feeble verbal examples, an eloquence vacuum exists that no rules and theory of writing, no discussion of motifs and metaphors, no vocabulary lists can easily fill.

A student's language ability can be seriously corrupted by listening to the colloquial, malformed, disconnected ramblings which dominate everyday speech and which blatantly violate the SAT language rule set with relentless consistency. There are, however, sources of good language online which parallel formal written English very closely. Never dreamt of just a few years ago, audio and video feeds of everything from audio books, news reports and lectures to debates, discussion, drama, and even formal instruction on every conceivable subject are accessible either freely or at least economically on the Internet.

A repository of free university resources and spoken English example videos has been compiled for this book.

University websites, particularly MIT, Annenberg, and Cambridge University have published vast libraries of lectures, debates and interviews from which the student can learn the sound and feel of well-spoken English.

The public school child cannot escape the sounds of sloppy language, but its influence can be somewhat softened by the introduction of material which can improve the influences to which a learner is subjected. Of course, the example set by the parents is the best place to start.

A Few Very Useful Resources
(*See* Online Resources p273)

- Princeton online archived lectures
- Online courses at Yale University
- Harvard @ Home
- Itunes of classes and lectures at Stanford
- British Academy Lectures online
- Video and audio from the University of Cambridge: Distinguished lectures
- Podcasts from the University of Oxford
- The British Academy John Locke Lecture Series
- The University of Oxford on iTunes U
- Massachusetts Institute of Technology: MIT World

Subjunctive Voice

There are two main forms of subjunctive in the English language, the present and past subjunctive. These really have nothing to do with points in the passage of time however. They simply mean different things.

Subjunctive verb forms can be used by the speaker or writer to convey another sense of verb action besides the simple declarative indicative form. They are used to imply that the action is conditional or entirely hypothetical or that it is a demand or supposition. The past form is normally reserved for referring to untrue or non-factual instances.

Past Subjunctive

Past subjunctive is used when the speaker wishes to indicate that the action described is hypothetical, is contrafactual, is untrue – a situation contrary to fact.   All forms of the verb "be" become "were". Other verbs use the past tense, or if already in past tense, the past perfect tense.

For example:

Indicative:

> *If he **was** thinking about what he was doing, he would put the lid on in time.*   (He may have been thinking)

Subjunctive:

> *If he **were** thinking about what he was doing...*   (He clearly wasn't thinking about it).
>
> *If he **had been** thinking about what he was doing...* (subjunctive in past becomes past perfect).

The past subjunctive is also used in a future sense:

> ***Were** he to paint it blue first thing in the morning, it might appear intentional.*

The speaker can choose to use or not to use subjunctive to convey either a fictive or factual impression.

As "were" is already the verb form for second person and plural of the verb "be" in past tense, the presence of the subjunctive is only clear in first and third person singular:

Indicative:

> *The lieutenant **was** anxious about the laundry.*

Subjunctive:

> *If the lieutenant **were** anxious about the laundry he would have put out the platypus.*

Indicative:

> *I **am** thinking clearly and do it for him.*

Subjunctive:

> *If I **were** thinking clearly I would do it for him.*
>
> *If I **had been**   thinking clearly I would have done it for him.*

Present Subjunctive

The present subjunctive is used in an order, a request, a decree, or in an "if" clause that is not necessarily contrafactual.

Indicative:

> *Uncle Cuthbert **is***

Present subjunctive

> *Aunt Agatha demanded that Uncle Cuthbert **be** present at the embalming ceremony.*
>
> *We could all go home if this **be** indeed the rabbit we're looking for.*
>
> *Boadicea requested that we all **be** upstanding when we sing the chorus of the prenuptial agreement.*
>
> *It was suggested that he **have** his turn-of-the-century diving equipment handy.*

The subjunctive verb form is distinguishable from the indicative only in specific cases. In the third person singular of most verbs in the present tense, this is done by omitting the "s". For example:

Indicative:

> *The tutor **complains, shouts** and **equivocates**.*

Subjunctive:

*Rupert demanded that he **complain, shout** and **equivocate** quietly.*

Present subjunctive of the verb "be" is 'very obvious, the indicative form of the verb is simply replaced with "be":

Indicative:
> *I **am**,*
> *you **are***
> *she **is***
> *we **are***
> *they **are**   going to the Pixley Festival of Disagreeable Cheeses.*

Subjunctive:
The handout demanded that
> *I **be***
> *You **be***
> *She **be***
> *We **be***
> *They **be** present at the launching of the Catatonic Cormorant instead.*

Subjunctive Playsheet

Choose the correct verb form.
1. Juliette reluctantly decreed, through billows of acrid polyester fumes, that stuffed toys [are, be, were] prevented from playing with the waffle iron.

2. A rather threadbare terrycloth squid avoided Juliette's gaze lest it [is, be, were] prevented from reaching the toaster oven.

3. If only Boadicea [is, was, were, would be] able to extract the squid from the vacuum cleaner, we should have a breakfast to remember.

4. The tides would be far greater if the moon [was, were] made of Camembert or Brie rather than Romano.

5. If it could be determined that the meteor actually [was, were] composed of gorgonzola, we would know a great deal more about the nature of life in the universe than we currently do.

6. The irascible Cossack demanded that the ironmonger [produce, produces] 16 hand-wrought Sicilian trivets.

7. The beast in the hamper produced an exhalation of green vapor as if it [be, was, were] a flatulent dimetrodon.

8. If the beast in the hamper [is, be, was, were] a dimetrodon, then this egg should not be kept in the refrigerator.

9. The baffled cormorant noted that the eels [were, be, are] served with vegemite.

10. Rupert took exception to the demand that he [relinquish, relinquishes, relinquished] his fleet in the Adriatic.

11. Perhaps Aunt Agatha would come out of the wardrobe if Rupert [is, was, were] to flush the fireworks down the euphemism.

12. Uncle Cuthbert has a profound fear of postage stamps, [are, were, is, be] they foreign, domestic, canceled, or not.

13. The officious vice principal demanded that all pencil sharpeners [are, were, be, is] confiscated and that papers henceforth were, are, be written in crayon on linoleum.

14. In her third attempt to arrange the class seating chart, Gloria decreed that nobody [sits, sat, sit] beside the person next to him or her.

15. If that [was, were, would be, is] the loathsome profligate you saw in the seaweed emporium on Sunday, he can't be held responsible for the affair involving the incontinent ruminant.

Answers

1. Juliette reluctantly decreed, through billows of acrid polyester fumes, that stuffed toys be prevented from playing with the waffle iron.

2. A rather threadbare terrycloth squid avoided Juliette's gaze lest it be prevented from reaching the toaster oven.

3. If only Boadicea were able to extract the squid from the vacuum cleaner, we should have a breakfast to remember.

4. The tides would be far greater if the moon [were, was] made of Camembert or Brie rather than Romano. (The choice of "was" or "were" depends on whether the speaker intends to imply that it is possible or not.)

5. If it could be determined that the meteor actually [was, were] composed of gorgonzola, we would know a great deal more about the nature of life in the universe than we currently do. (Again, both choices are possible depending upon the speaker's intent.)

6. The irascible Cossack demanded that the ironmonger produce 16 hand-wrought Sicilian trivets.

7. The beast in the hamper produced an exhalation of green vapor as if it were a flatulent dimetrodon.

8. If the beast in the hamper [was, were] a dimetrodon, then this egg should not be kept in the refrigerator. (Again, both choices are possible depending upon the speaker's intent.)

9. The baffled cormorant noted that the eels were served with vegemite. (There is no subjunctive in this case. Were the cormorant to demand that the eels be served with vegemite, there would be.)

10. Rupert took exception to the demand that he relinquish his fleet in the Adriatic.

11. Perhaps Aunt Agatha would come out of the wardrobe if Rupert were to flush the fireworks down the euphemism.

12. Uncle Cuthbert has a profound fear of postage stamps, be they foreign, domestic, canceled, or not.

13. The officious vice principal demanded that all pencil sharpeners be confiscated and that papers henceforth be written in crayon on linoleum.

14. In her third attempt to arrange the class seating arrangement, Gloria decreed that nobody sit beside the person next to him or her.

15. If that was the loathsome profligate you saw in the seaweed emporium on Sunday, he can't be held responsible for the affair involving the incontinent ruminant. (No subjunctive here as it is not clearly a situation contrary to fact.)

Projects

1. Rewrite *Cinderella* in other words using synonyms from the glossary.

2. Describe the most repellant person you know personally and an experience that might be of benefit to him/her if it could be arranged.

3. Listen to an online lecture by Terry Eagleton (*See* Online Resources p273) and transcribe a few paragraphs. Note his use of metaphor, subjunctive and his general use of language.

Chapter 9

Vocabulary: The Fox, the Owl, and the Spinach Lasagna

In the tiny hamlet of Binge, there once lived an **agoraphobic** Fox named Festus who roomed with a **petulant** owl named Aloysius. Once, while **perusing** some ancient volumes, he happened across a **papyrus** manuscript, which, when closely examined, appeared to contain a recipe for spinach lasagna which **purported** to have magical medicinal curative powers over all manner of ailments. Festus set about to produce a batch of this **gustatory panacea** and put the kitchen into a state of **unmitigated pandemonium** in the attempt. Ingredients were somewhat hard to come by, as Aloysius was more than usually **parsimonious** for an owl with a **pecuniary** surplus, an unfortunate **paradox** under the circumstances.

The **pedantic** Aloysius had a **penchant** for the **sardonic** and ridiculed the entire undertaking, **parodying** Festus at every turn. Undeterred by temporary **penury** and Aloysius' **perfidy**, Festus succeeded in his venture. When faced with the

agoraphobic adj. frightened of open spaces

petulant adj. irritable

peruse v. To read with great care

papyrus n. ancient writing paper

purport v profess, intend, purpose

gustatory adj. tasty

panacea n. cure-all

unmitigated adj. unreduced

pandemonium n. confusion

parsimonious adj. stingy

pecuniary adj. related to money

paradox adj. contradiction

pedantic adj. doctrinaire

penchant n. inclination

sardonic adj. bitingly sarcastic

parody v. to ridicule through imitation

penury n. poverty

perfidy n. treachery

delectable aroma of the feast, even Aloysius was unable to resist and partook largely of the **repast**. Whatever other effects the meal might have had, it seemed to stifle all criticism in any who ate of it. Festus was elevated to **patriarch** of Binge by a substantial **plurality** the following year and Aloysius was duly **penitent**.

repast n. meal

patriarch n. male leader
plurality n. greater number
   of votes
penitent adj. remorseful

Glossary

agoraphobia n. Fear of open spaces. Agoraphobic adj.

gustatory adj. Of or relating to the sense of taste.

panacea n. A remedy or medicine proposed for or professing to cure all diseases; cure-all, solution.

pandemonium n. A fiendish or riotous uproar; chaos, bedlam, uproar. Pandemoniac adj.

papyrus n. The writing-paper of the ancient Egyptians, and later of the Romans.

paradox n. A statement or doctrine seemingly in contradiction to the received belief; contradiction, inconsistency, irony. Paradoxical adj.

parody v./n. To render ludicrous by imitating the language of; caricature, satire, spoof.

parsimonious adj. Excessively sparing in the use or expenditure of money; thrifty, frugal, miserly. Parsimony n.

patriarch n. The chief of a tribe or race who rules by paternal right. Patriarchal adj.

patronymic adj./n. Formed after one's father's name.   A name formed after one's father's name.

pecuniary adj. Consisting of or related to money; financial, fiscal, economic.

pedant n. A scholar who makes needless and inappropriate display of his learning; sophist. Pedantic adj. Pedantry n.

pedantic adj. Doctrinaire, sophistic, finicky, arcane.

penchant [for] n. Inclination [to, for], proclivity [for, to], affinity [for, to], predilection [for], fondness [for, of].

penitence n. Sorrow for a sin with desire to amend and to atone; contrition, repentance, remorse. Penitent adj.

penury n. Indigence, poverty, destitution. Penurious adj.

perfidy n. Treachery, disloyalty, deceit, betrayal. Perfidious adj.

peruse v. To read or examine with great care; to observe. Perusable adj. Perusal n.

petulant adj. Irritable, grouchy, ill-tempered, irascible, querulous. Petulance n.

plurality n. A majority (not really – the greatest number of votes
    cast for one of three or more candidates, but not a majori-
    ty of total votes cast)
purport v./n. To have the intention of doing; profess, purpose
repast n. Meal, banquet, buffet, feast, collation.
unmitigated adj. Undiminished, unreduced.
    Ant. mitigated. Mitigate v.

Quiz

1. Festus
    A. was a petulant owl.
    B. was afraid of open spaces.
    C. was generous.
    D. was fond of papyrus.

2. The papyrus manuscript
    A. was inedible.
    B. had curative powers.
    C. contained a recipe.
    D. contained a gustatory panacea.

3. The gustatory panacea
    A. was a spinach lasagna.
    B. had a penchant for the sardonic.
    C. was parsimonious.
    D. was pedantic.

4. Aloysius
    A. created the pandemonium.
    B. had all manner of ailments.
    C. was wealthy.
    D. perused some ancient volumes.

5. Festus
   A. created the pandemonium.
   B. had all manner of ailments.
   C. was wealthy.
   D. was afraid of spiders.

6. Festus
   A. was bitingly sarcastic.
   B. was treacherous.
   C. succeeded in his venture.
   D. was wealthy.

7. The feast
   A. produced temporary penury.
   B. was sardonic.
   C. was parsimonious.
   D. had a delectable aroma.

8. Aloysius
   A. was sorry for his behavior.
   B. was elected patriarch of Binge.
   C. stifled all criticism.
   D. had a delectable aroma.

Answers

1. B.
2. C.
3. A.
4. C.
5. A.
6. C.
7. D.
8. A.

Language Notes

Common Errors: Troubles with Case

In English, only pronouns are declined to indicate whether they are the subject or object of a verb. Other nouns do not change.

Pronoun Declension

number	person	gender*	pronouns	
			subject	object
singular	1st	m/f	I	me
	2nd	m/f	you	you
	3rd	m	he	him
		f	she	her
		n	it	it
plural	1st	m/f	we	us
	2nd	m/f	you	you
	3rd	m/f/n	they	them
s/p	3rd	m/f	who	whom

* m=masculine f=feminine n=neuter

Following the pronoun chart above, *I, he, she, we, they*, and *who* can serve as verb subjects only. Your ear tells you that *I saw she* or *I talked to they* are wrong and that the pronouns must be replaced by objective case pronouns *her* and *them* respectively: *I saw her* and *I talked with them*.

It is harder to determine which of *who* and *whom* should be used as *who* is commonly used in everyday speech where *whom* would be correct. Nonetheless, one should use *whom* where it is called for in formal speech or writing. It is often easiest to tell which is right by substituting *he* for *who* and *him* for *whom* as the ear is better attuned to them.

Wrong:

> *Who should we ask to sponsor Rupert into the Union of Concerned Miscreants and Scoundrels?*

Find the subject, verb, and object and determine whether the pronoun is used as a subject or an object. Ask yourself whether *he* or *him* fits best:

> *Should we ask he?*
> *Should we ask him?*

If the answer is *he*, then replace it with *who*.
If the answer is *him*, then replace it with *whom*.

In this case, the object of the verb *ask* would clearly be *him*, and therefore *whom*.

> *Whom should we ask to sponsor Rupert into the Union of Concerned Miscreants and Scoundrels?*

In statements in which a comparison is made using *than* or *as*, the following word is a nominative subject:

> *Nobody could possibly be as scrofulous as he.*
> *Under no circumstances could Rupert show more blatant disregard than I.*

The *he* and *I* above are regarded as subjects of a missing but implied verb:

> *Nobody could possibly be as scrofulous as he (is).*
> *Under no circumstances could Rupert show more blatant disregard than I (show).*

When a pronoun follows *as* or *than*, check to see if a verb could be given to the pronoun and if so, use the nominative form of the pronoun. Although this is clearly correct, analysis of web usage shows that this correct use does seem to be outweighed by misusages. (*See* The World's Largest Usage Dictionary p12)

Case Quiz

Some of the following contain subject/object errors. Circle the errors or indicate their absence. Below each error, write your corrected version.

First, identify pronouns whose case must be reflected correctly. Check if they are the subject or object of a verb. Look for elliptical constructs using *as* or *than*, and prepositions that may take the pronoun as an object.

Example:
> *Who should we expect to weave the missing chocolate birdbath into the conversation before she forgets to do anything useful with the document shredder or the pot of experimental begonias?*

subject	verb	object
We	should expect	who/whom

Again, it is often best to replace who/whom pairs with he/him pairs as the ear is more attuned to them:

subject	verb	object
We	should expect	he

Clearly, *we should expect he* is wrong and should be *we should expect him* and therefore, *we should expect whom*. Thus, corrected, the sentence would read:

> *Whom should we expect to weave the missing chocolate birdbath into the conversation before she forgets to do an-*

ything useful with the document shredder or the pot of experimental begonias?

1. Severus asked the three braves and I whether a greased ferret might stand a chance of fetching the broken spectacles.

2. Boadicea doubted that anyone could be quite as excited as her when Gerald tried tying the herring tarts to the paddle and dipping them in the marmalade.

3. Rowena and Boadicea assured the artist that nobody in the kingdom could possibly fling yogurt more gracefully or with more sublime effect than him.

4. Neither Rowland nor Boadicea, emerging slowly from behind the inflatable hyena, could imagine anyone irritating the postman as artfully as they.

5. Whom should be expected to unload the amorous giraffe before the rain washes all the fudge away revealing the magic tortoise and the baseball cap.

6. Neither the dwarf on the tricycle nor me could be seen clearly behind the smoldering bagpipes – or it is to be sincerely hoped that we could not.

7. Even these strangely loony Hungarians could suspect neither the ornately painted guests nor I of hiding the recalcitrant ostrich in our luggage.

8. Only when accompanied by the troubadour, the two thoroughly inebriated ice-cream salesmen, and me, did Hermione stand a chance of intimidating the officious, flowerpot-wielding zookeeper.

9. Several counterfeit reproductions of the statue were discovered by the archivist and I after Hermione pried the cellar door open with an industrial-strength spurtle and we started rummaging through the egg cartons.

Answers

1. Severus asked the three braves and I whether a greased ferret might stand a chance of fetching the broken spectacles.   **Pronoun: I/me**
   Severus asked me **is clearly best as** *me* **is the object of the verb** *ask.*   **Thus: Severus asked the three braves and me whether a greased ferret might stand a chance of fetching the broken spectacles.**

subject	verb	object
Severus	asked	me

2. Boadicea doubted that anyone could be quite as excited as her when Gerald tried tying the herring tarts to the paddle and dipping them in the marmalade.
   Pronoun: she.
   Note the word *as* **which makes this an elliptical construct with missing verb could: Boadicea doubted that anyone could be quite as excited as she (could).**

subject	verb
she	could

3. Rowena and Boadicea assured the artist that nobody in the kingdom could possibly fling yogurt more gracefully or with more sublime effect than him.
   Pronoun: him.
   Note the word *than* **which makes this an elliptical construct with implied verb** *could.*   **... could fling yogurt as...as he (could).**

subject	verb
he	could

4. Neither Rowland nor Boadicea, emerging slowly from behind the inflatable hyena, could imagine anyone irritating the postman as artfully as they.

Pronoun: they. This is an elliptical construct with implied verb *could*.   Neither Rowland nor Boadicea, emerging slowly from behind the inflatable hyena, could imagine anyone irritating the postman as artfully as they (could). This sentence is correct as it is.

subject	verb
they	could

5. Whom should be expected to unload the amorous giraffe before the rain washes all the fudge away revealing the magic tortoise and the baseball cap.

Pronoun: whom.

Who should be **clearly sounds better as *who* is the subject of the verb, thus: Who should be expected to unload the amorous giraffe before the rain washes all the fudge away revealing the magic tortoise and the baseball cap.**

subject	verb
Who	should be expected

6. Neither the dwarf on the tricycle nor me could be seen clearly behind the smoldering bagpipes – or it is to be sincerely hoped that we could not.

Pronoun: me

I could be **clearly sounds better as *I* is the subject of the verb *could,* thus: Neither the dwarf on the tricycle nor I could be seen clearly behind the smoldering bagpipes – or it is to be sincerely hoped that we could not. (*We* is also an inflected pronoun but is clearly correct as the subject of the verb could: we could not.)**

subject	verb
I	could be

7. Even these strangely loony Hungarians could suspect neither the ornately painted guests nor I of hiding the recalcitrant ostrich in our luggage.

Pronoun: I

The pronoun is the object of the verb phrase *could suspect*, and must therefore be *me*:   Even these strangely loony Hungarians could suspect neither the ornately painted guests nor me of hiding the recalcitrant ostrich in our luggage.

subject	verb	object
Hungarians	could suspect	me

8. Only when accompanied by the troubadour, the two thoroughly inebriated ice-cream salesmen and me, did Hermione stand a chance of intimidating the officious flowerpot-wielding zookeeper.

Pronoun: Me

The passive verb construct uses the preposition *by* and the pronoun is the object of the preposition. Thus, the use of *me* is correct: Only when accompanied by the troubadour, the two thoroughly inebriated ice-cream salesmen, and me, did Hermione stand a chance of intimidating the officious flowerpot-wielding zookeeper.

subject	verb	preposition	object of preposition
Hermione	(was) accompanied	by	me

9. Several counterfeit reproductions of the statue were discovered by the archivist and I after Hermione pried the cellar door open with an industrial-strength spurtle and we started rummaging through the egg cartons.

Pronoun: I

The passive verb construct uses the preposition *by* and the pronoun is the object of the preposition. Thus it should be *by me*: Several counterfeit reproductions of the statue were discovered by the archivist and me after Hermione pried

the cellar door open with an industrial-strength spurtle and we started rummaging through the egg cartons.

subject	verb	preposition	object of pre-position
reproductions	were dis-covered	by	me

Who and Whom

It is harder to determine which of *who* and *whom* should be used as *who* is commonly used in everyday speech where *whom* would be correct. Nonetheless, one should use *whom* where it is called for in formal speech or writing. It is often easiest to tell which is right by substituting *he* for *who* and *him* for *whom* as the ear is better attuned to them.

Wrong:

> *Who should we ask to sponsor Rupert into the Union of Concerned Miscreants and Scoundrels?*

Find the subject, verb, and object and determine whether the pronoun is used as a subject or an object. Ask yourself whether *he* or *him* fits best:

> *Should we ask he?*
> *Should we ask him?*

If the answer is *he*, then replace it with *who*.
If the answer is *him*, then replace it with *whom*.

In this case, the object of the verb *ask* would clearly be *him*, and therefore *whom*.

> *Whom should we ask to sponsor Rupert into the Union of Concerned Miscreants and Scoundrels?*

Choose the Correct Who/Whom Pronoun

1. I don't know _____ the paste-encrusted soup bowl belongs to. Give it to _____ever comes out of the library holding a spoon.

2. She gave the musical score to the prenuptial agreement to Rupert and _____ else? _____ should perform it for the board and _____ do you think should be blamed for the idea if they walk out in the middle?

3. _____ did you consider to be the least likely to approach aunt Agatha about the earring in the salad? She is not likely to be pleased with _____ever we pick to break the news to her.

4. Would _____ever found my copy of "Ethel, the Exculpated Aardvark" please return it to Mr. Thackeray's mailbox with a note of apology.

5. Would _____ever the statuary director designated, please re-place Prometheus' sword and remove the kangaroo?

6. Would _____ever put the Jello on the table of the last supper tableau please return the fish?

7. Hermione presented the briefly used mustard container to the sixth-grader _____ Stephen had accused of artistic debau-chery.

8. She gave the rapidly rotting onion to the student _____ was chosen to be the standard bearer.

9. She gave the spear to the one _____ the giant frog seemed to like best.

10. Few members of the committee had yet had occasion to visit with the nurse _____ the kindergarten class had dubbed "Fla-tula".

11. Understanding the prefect _____ wore the diplodocus suit was not easy for those _____ Mrs. Muffet had seated in the balcony behind the pasta nativity.

Answers

1. whom, who
2. whom, who, who
3. whom, whom
4. who
5. whom
6. who
7. whom
8. who
9. whom
10. whom
11. who, whom

Harder Who/Whom Practice

Fill in the blank with Who or Whom as appropriate.

1. _____ did the mural of downtown Pasadena infested with Frisbee-throwing kangaroos most effectively irritate?

2. _____ did this exemplary book report on The History of Footwear in Estonia in crayon?

3. _____ do you think should recite Dr. Seuss's Lorax while balancing the barbaloots and juggling thneeds?

4. _____ shall we have recite Dr. Seuss's Lorax while balancing the barbaloots and juggling the thneeds?

5. _____ did the mural of downtown Pasadena infested with Frisbee-throwing kangaroos?

6. _____ do you consider to be the least objectionable representative from the Monrovia chapter of the Union of Concerned Miscreants and Scoundrels?

7. _____ did this exemplary book report on The History of Footwear in Estonia?

8. _____ is the most inconspicuous member of the Clockwork Submarine Enthusiast's Amateur Operatic Society likely to impersonate?

9. After doing the Louvre, _____ did the Museum of the Shoes of Famous Frenchmen?

10. _____, do you think, would be the least objectionable representative from the Monrovia chapter of the Union of Concerned Miscreants and Scoundrels?

11. _____ had the enormous melting snow diplodocus with him when he crept through the rumpus room and over the nearly new Persian carpet?

12. _____ did this exemplary book report on The History of Footwear in Estonia intimidate?

13. _____ had the enormous melting snow diplodocus soaked when creeping through the rumpus room and over the nearly new Persian carpet?

14. After doing the Louvre, _____ did the Museum of the Shoes of Famous Frenchmen cause to lose all sensation in her left heel?

15. _____ is the most inconspicuous member of the Clockwork Submarine Enthusiast's Amateur Operatic Society?

Answers

1.	whom	8.	whom
2.	who	9.	who
3.	who	10.	who
4.	whom	11.	who
5.	who	12.	whom
6.	whom	13.	whom
7.	who	14.	whom

Projects

1. Consider the statement: *We are forced to judge students by the courses they have taken and the grades they have received rather than by their knowledge and competence.* Is this the best criterion by which to judge students? Take a position on the best way or ways to assess student achievement and write the rough draft of a paper to support your decision. Give examples and justify your conclusions.

2. Write an imaginative and highly detailed recipe for a dish you would probably be unwilling to eat yourself. Make it as convincing as possible, share it with friends (and, perhaps, those less friendly) and write down and interpret the responses you receive, rating them for intelligence, sincerity and bad taste.

Chapter 10

Vocabulary: The Bat and the Sandwich, Part 1

Bucephalus Bat read with **relish** the notice posted high in the forest canopy for the benefit of **arboreal** animals. The coming fair **conjured** up wistful and **nostalgic** images of food, games, and **diversions** in his mind. An **astute** observer of **parental predilections**, he **anticipated** that the coming event would at best **elicit** a **stolid apathetic** response from them or, at worst, **repudiation, acerbity** and sarcasm. Fearing the latter case and a **debacle** that could result in his having to **forgo** participation, he **broached** the subject with delicacy, characterizing the event as **innocuous** and **insipid**, knowing well the **proclivity** of his parents for (in his view) **vapidity** and tedium. For a moment it appeared that he would have to **forbear** partaking of the festivities and, **envious, galled** in the extreme, and **bemoaning** his **genealogy**, be forced to listen to his friends **extolling** the delights of the fair in past tense. **Tenacity** won out however, and his appeal, **inexplicably, educed implicit** consent.

relish n. delight
arboreal adj. tree dwelling
conjure v. call up
nostalgic adj. fond longing
diversion n. amusement
astute adj. observant
parental adj. of parents
predilection n. inclination
anticipate v. expect
elicit v. bring forth
stolid adj. emotionless
apathetic adj. unconcerned
repudiation n. disavowal
acerbity n. sourness
debacle n. fiasco
forgo v. refrain from
broach v. mention
innocuous adj. bland   insipid adj. dull
proclivity n. inclination
vapidity n. lack of interest
forbear v. refrain from
envious adj. desirous
gall v. irritate
bemoan v. lament
genealogy n. lineage
extol v. admire

Central to the **revelry** would be a show at which all manner of art, crafts, produce, and performance art would be judged in one vast **heterogeneous melee** of **disparate** accomplishments. His **coterie convened surreptitiously** beside the wobbly dum dum bush beneath the magic oak tree to **confer** upon and exchange strategies for the

tenacity n. determination
inexplicable adj. mysterious
educe v. evoke
implicit adj. implied
revelry n. festivities
heterogeneous adj. assorted
melee n. tussle
disparate adj. different
coterie n. select group
convene v. meet
surreptitious adj. sneaky
confer v. discuss

show. Baby bear, renowned for his **resplendent** artistic constructions, had long since decided upon a **replica** of castle Neuschwanstein done entirely in **desiccated** condensed cream of mushroom soup. The group generally regarded Baby Bear's **prowess** with the trowel and palette knife as **virtually unassailable** but, however **precocious** he might be, his **preoccupation** with **unorthodox** media might well work to his **detriment** in the judging – if indeed the **opus** lasted long enough to be judged at all. Clearly, there was room in the field for other **aspirants**.

The **chandlery** of Wee Willie Winkie was a **perennial** entry. Always **tawdry** and **ostentatious**, it could not be overlooked, however much one might try. The floral grandeur of Mary Quite Contrary's entry would certainly place it in contention, as would the **cucurbitic** majesty of Peter Peter Pumpkin Eater's construction grade vegetables. The **aquatic** mammals had decided to **choreograph** and perform a water ballet but were undecided as to whether the siege of Troy or a **chronology** of the decline of the Roman Empire would best **fadge** with their talents and medium. One small penguin also had the **audacity** to **persevere** in his proposal for the reenactment of an undocumented conflict between Vikings and Amazons.

resplendent adj. dazzling
replica n. facsimile

desiccated adj. dried
prowess n. expertise
virtual adj. effective
unassailable adj. undeniable
precocious adj. talented
preoccupation n. obsession
unorthodox adj. unconventional
detriment n. disadvantage
opus n. artistic work
aspirant n. contender
chandlery n. candle-making business
perennial adj. lasting
tawdry adj. cheap, flashy
ostentatious adj. pretentious
cucurbitic adj. related to pumpkins

aquatic adj. water
choreograph v. compose dance steps
chronology n. time line

fadge v. to suit

audacity n. boldness
persevere v. to persist

Bucephalus was still **perplexed** as to what form his contribution should take. He refused to be **stereotyped** by **genus**-specific **prejudices**. Indeed, he did not suffer from a **dearth** of choices. He was an accomplished **raconteur** with a flourishing vegetable garden, could walk a tightrope comfortably (up-side down while juggling root vegetables), and was highly **enamored** of the **culinary** arts, particularly **confections** and sauces. Thus, he was lost in **ambivalence** even about the field he should choose. Upon reflection, an alternative occurred to him. Why should he choose at all? Could he not devise an intersection of produce and preserves with culinary and performance art? And why not sculpture, choreography, and story-telling as well? Would the judges be **libertarian** enough to consider such an entry?

perplex v. confuse

stereotype v. pigeonhole
genus n. category
prejudice n. intolerance
dearth n. lack
raconteur n. story teller

enamored [of] adj. in love with
culinary adj. of cooking
confection n. sweet things
ambivalence n. indecision

libertarian adj. tolerant

Glossary

ambivalence n. Uncertainty or indecisiveness about which of multiple courses to follow; indecision, dubiety, ambiguity. Ambivalent adj.
anticipate v. To feel or realize in advance; expect, foresee, predict, await. Anticipatory adj.
apathetic adj. Unconcerned, indifferent; listless. Apathy n.
aquatic adj./n. Of or pertaining to water or the sea; marine.
arboreal adj. Of, pertaining to, or living in a tree or trees; sylvan.
acerbity n. Sourness of character, appearance, or tone; acidity, acrimony, asperity, astringency, tartness. Acerbic adj.

aspire v. To have a great ambition or goal; seek, aim, hope, wish.
Aspirant n.

aspirant n. One who aspires; candidate, applicant, contender.
Aspire v.

astute adj. Observant, keen, perceptive, perspicacious, shrewd,
incisive. Astuteness n.

audacious adj. Foolhardy, daring, brave, bold, impudent, risky.
Audacity n.

audacity n. Daring, boldness, courage, nerve, impudence.
Audacious adj.

bemoan v. To express grief over; lament, bewail, regret, mourn.

broach v. To bring up [a subject] for discussion or consideration;
mention, raise.

chandlery n. Candle wares or wares sold by a chandler; a store-
room where candles are kept

chandler n. One who makes and sells candles.

choreograph v. To formulate movement sequences as in dance;
design, plan, direct.

chronological adj. Sequential, ordered as in a timeline.
Chronology n.

chronology n. A time line or time-ordered sequence.
Chronological adj.

confer v. To discuss. To engage in conference. Conference n.

confer v. To give, to bestow upon; award, present, grant.
Conferment n. Conferrable adj.

conjure (up) v. Call up; invoke, summon.

confection n. A sweet preparation such as candy.

convene v. To assemble, to meet as a group; summon, call together.

coterie n. A small, often select, group of persons who meet frequently for a purpose; click, assemblage.

curcubita n. The genus to which pumpkins belong. Curcurbitic
and curcubitive are adjectival forms of curcubita.

culinary adj. Of or relating to the art of food preparation; cooking, cookery, gustatory.

dearth n. Scarcity, paucity, lack, shortage, insufficiency, deficiency.

debacle n. Fiasco, catastrophe, disaster, shambles, tragedy, calamity.

desiccated adj. Dried out; shriveled, dehydrated, shrunken. Desiccate v.

detriment n. Harm, damage, disadvantage disparagement. Detrimental adj.

disparate adj. Of differing kind, having dissimilar properties; contrasting, distinct, divergent, inconsistent, unequivalent.

diversion n. The act of turning aside from ones path or a distracting entertainment; distraction, amusement, recreation. Diversionary adj.

educe v. Bring forth; elicit, conclude, evoke, obtain. Educible adj. Eduction n.

elicit v. Bring forth, obtain, extract, educe. Elicitation n.

enamor v. To inspire with love. [*To be enamored of* is *to be in love with*]

envious adj. Feeling, expressing or characterized by envy; covetous, desirous.

envy n. Jealousy, covetousness. Envious adj.

extol v. Admire, praise, exalt. Extolment n.

fadge v. To suit, match, or be appropriate; to fit with.

forbear v. Hold back, abstain, refrain from.

forgo v. Abstain from; give up, relinquish, decline.

gall v. Irritate, provoke, infuriate.
n. nerve, impudence, audacity.

genealogy n. Familial ancestry, pedigree, descent, lineage. Genealogical adj.

genus n. A biological category, a level of the taxonomic hierarchy more specific than family but more general than species. Pl. genera.

heterogeneous adj. Composed of elements with different properties; varied, assorted, various, mixed, non-uniform, dissimilar. Heterogeneity n.

implicit adj. Understood, unspoken, implied, couched, inherent, embedded. Imply v.

inexplicable adj. Mysterious, enigmatic, baffling, incomprehensible, bizarre. Inexplicability n.

innocuous adj. Harmless, inoffensive, innocent, mild, bland, vapid, insipid, jejune, tedious, uninspiring, vacant, vacuous.

insipid adj. Dull, characterless, wishy-washy, innocuous.
    Insipidity adj.

libertarian adj./n. Tolerant, permissive, broadminded.

melee n. A confused battle; brawl, clash, fracas, fray, tussle.

nostalgia n. A fond longing for things of the past; reminiscence, wistfulness, longing. Nostalgic adj.

opus n. An artistic creation; composition, work, piece.

opera n. Plural of opus, a work. A dramatic work incorporating music and singing.

ostentation n. Showiness, affectation, flamboyance, pretension. Ostentatious adj.

ostentatious adj. Displaying wealth; pretentious, showy, boastful, affected, grandiose, flamboyant. Ostentation n.

parental adj. Of or relating to parenthood. Parent n.

perennial adj./n. Enduring; recurrent, permanent, returning, lasting, persistent.

perplex v. Baffle, bewilder, confuse, confound, stymie, puzzle. Perplexity n.

persevere v. To persist in one's purpose.

precocious adj. Talented beyond one's age; gifted, intelligent, talented. Precocity n.

predilection n. Inclination, tendency, partiality, penchant, preference.

prejudice n. Intolerance, chauvinism, bigotry. Prejudicial adj.

preoccupation n. Obsession, fixation. Preoccupy v.

proclivity n. Inclination, taste, penchant, predilection.

prowess n. Skill or ability; expertise, competence, proficiency.

raconteur n. Story teller.

relish v./n. Like, delight in, enjoy.

replica n. A copy or reproduction; imitation, model, facsimile, duplication. Replicate v.

repudiate v. To refuse to have anything to do with; reject, cast off, disclaim, disavow, renounce. Repudiation n.

repudiation n. The act of repudiating.

resplendent adj. Magnificent, brilliant, glorious, dazzling, stunning. Resplendence n.

revelry n. Enthusiastic merrymaking; festivities, celebrations, partying. Revelrous adj.

stereotype v. Pigeonhole, typecast, categorize. Stereotypic adj. Stereotypical adj.

n. An example of stereotyping.

stolid adj. Dull, emotionless, unresponsive. Stolidity n.

surreptitious adj. Clandestine, stealthy, furtive, secret, sneaky, covert.

tawdry adj./n. Flashy, cheap, tasteless.

tenacity n. Persistence, determination, stubbornness, obstinacy, doggedness, resolve. Tenacious adj.

unassailable adj. Undeniable, incontrovertible, unquestionable, irrefutable, indisputable. Unassailability n.

unorthodox adj. Diverging from established practice; unconventional, untraditional, nonconformist. Unorthodoxy n.

vapidity n. Lacking interest; commonplace, insipidity. Vapid adj.

virtual adj. Existing in effect but not in actual fact; effective, practical, essential. Virtuality n.

Quiz

1. The notice posted in the forest canopy
    A. was placed there for flying animals.
    B. was placed there for tree-dwelling animals.
    C. was placed there for nostalgic animals.
    D. was placed there with relish.

2. Bucephalus
    A. studied closely the inclinations of his parents.
    B. was stolid and apathetic.
    C. conferred with his parents upon strategies for the show.
    D. was renowned for his artistic constructions.

3. The fair
   A. was for the benefit of arboreal animals.
   B. was vapid and tedious.
   C. was something Bucephalus did not want to miss.
   D. might have been cancelled.

4. There would be a contest at the fair
   A. for growers of vegetables.
   B. for acrobats.
   C. for thespians.
   D. open to all kinds of entries.

5. Bucephalus' group of friends
   A. met secretly.
   B. wore gaudy socks.
   C. was renowned for their sculpture.
   D. had a preoccupation with unorthodox media.

6. Wee Willie Winkie's candles
   A. were often overlooked.
   B. were often entered at the fair.
   C. were redolent.
   D. were simple and elegant.

7. Mary Quite Contrary
   A. was an aquatic mammal.
   B. lived in a pumpkin.
   C. reenacted an undocumented conflict between Vikings and Amazons.
   D. entered flowers at the fair.

8. Bucephalus
   A. grew construction-grade vegetables.
   B. was afraid of open spaces.
   C. could tell a good story.
   D. sided with the penguin.

9. Bucephalus
   A. wanted to juggle turnips and potatoes.
   B. could not make up his mind what to enter at the fair.
   C. disliked cooking.
   D. was stolid and apathetic.

10. Bucephalus and his coterie
   A. reenacted the siege of Troy.
   B. grew vegetables.
   C. admired Baby Bear's sculpting skills.
   D. admired Baby Bear's preoccupation with unorthodox media.

Answers

1. B.	6. B.
2. A.	7. D.
3. C.	8. C.
4. D.	9. B.
5. A.	10. C.

Language Notes

Common Errors: Modifiers

A pronoun must refer to a single noun, not a phrase or a collection of oddments and especially may not refer to nothing at all. Check your work to determine the reference for pronouns.

Wrong:

The accountant's wheelbarrow was full of eels, which irritated the fastidious spectator.

The *which* does not refer to a specific noun.

Better:

The presence of eels in the accountant's wheelbarrow irritated the fastidious spectator.

Quiz: Ambiguous or Unresolved References

Find and circle the ambiguous or unresolved references in the following.

1. The spinning wheel stood on the ancient parapet before it was dismantled.

2. The banner flew in the sparkling sun as the cavalcade approached the battlements just before it disappeared from view.

3. Harold helped Hermione rewrite the screenplay of *Delightful Moments with Hideous People* before being insulted by the dockworker, and it reminded her of a mermaid on a motorcycle.

4. While trying ineffectually to retrieve the eggplant centerpiece from his neighbor's trout pond, Rupert's phone wouldn't stop playing Monteverdi's Orfeo and the chicken just kept dancing until Irmgard threw a yogurt-encrusted spatula at him.

5. The day after the strange incident with the petulant penguin, Mabel found Hermione and Penelope putting the finishing touches on the marble bust of Jane Austin and then she came down with a bad cold and hid it in the refrigerator until she could think of a better way to explain why she missed the deadline.

6. There was a rumor going around that the library's copy of *16 More Things to Do in Zero Gravity* had been used to

store the desiccated duck's liver long after the expiry date and it was nasty.

7. The members of the sixth grade cooking class were issued charismatic wooden spoons, but were told by the three whisk-wielding Muscovites that they were expected to present them to the members of the board of holistic balloonists when they finished their tour of the campus model-railroader's exhibit of extinct Siberian waterfowl.

Answers

1. The spinning wheel stood on the ancient parapet before it was dismantled. **What was dismantled? The parapet? The spinning wheel?**

2. The banner flew in the sparkling sun as the cavalcade approached the battlements just before it disappeared from view. **What disappeared? The sun, cavalcade, banner?**

3. Harold helped Hermione rewrite the screenplay of *Delightful Moments with Hideous People* before being insulted by the dockworker, and it reminded her of a mermaid on a motorcycle. **Who was insulted? What reminded her of a mermaid on a motorcycle?**

4. While trying ineffectually to retrieve the eggplant centerpiece from his neighbor's trout pond, Rupert's phone wouldn't stop playing Monteverdi's Orfeo and the chicken just kept dancing until Irmgard threw a yogurt-encrusted spatula at him. **At whom did Irmgard throw the spatula? Rupert? Monteverdi? The Chicken?**

5. The day after the strange incident with the petulant penguin, Mabel found Hermione and Penelope putting the finishing touches on the marble bust of Jane Austin and then she came down with a bad cold and hid it in the refrigera-

tor until she could think of a better way to explain why she missed the deadline. **Who came down with a cold? Mabel? Hermione? Penelope? The bust? What was hidden in the refrigerator? The penguin? The cold? The bust?**

6. There was a rumor going around that the library's copy of *16 More Things to Do in Zero Gravity* had been used to store the desiccated duck's liver long after the expiry date and it was nasty. **What expiry date? The book? The Duck's liver? What was nasty? The rumor? The Library? The duck's liver? The book?**

7. The members of the sixth grade cooking class were issued charismatic wooden spoons, but were told by the three whisk-wielding Muscovites that they were expected to present them to the members of the board of holistic balloonists when they finished their tour of the campus model-railroader's exhibit of extinct Siberian waterfowl. **Who was expected to present whom? The members of the cooking class? The Muscovites? When who finished the tour?**

Misplaced Modifiers

Modifying phrases must modify something appropriate. "Misplaced" modifiers dangle about untidily. A participial phrase such as "having enraged the librarian" must refer to the subject of the following phrase: "having enraged the librarian, the three rebarbative itinerants were banned from the establishment" and not "having enraged the librarian, Mr. Wainwright banned the three rebarbative itinerants from the establishment" because Mr. Wainwright was not the one who did the enraging.

Here are some examples.

> *While climbing Mt. Kilimanjaro, which is quite steep up to the very top and then slopes away rather sharply, Rupert's hair dryer required constant adjustment.*

(Who is climbing the mountain? The hair drier?)

> *Ducking under a flock of pestilent soiled budgies, the handlebars struck the sandwich in my pocket doing irreparable harm to the avocado.*

(Who or what is ducking?)

> *To Rupert's surprise, he was comfortably able to drive the tractor wearing swim fins and goggles.*

(Is the tractor wearing swim fins and goggles?)

Modifiers and Antecedents Playsheet

Circle the ambiguities or unresolved references in the following or note that there is no error.

1. While perusing *Ethel the Aardvark on Differential Calculus*, nobody noticed the shoe salesman driving a compact car wearing a hat.

2. Being far too full to eat a bite more, the offer of Venezuelan beaver cheese did not evoke the expected howls of delight.

3. Unable to extract the squid from the vacuum cleaner, breakfast consisted only of eggs and aging Braunschweiger.

4. Ranging in size from that of a large hamster to that of three very small elk, I didn't know whether to look for them in the grass, up a tree, or under a bridge.

5. After constructing the elaborate pasta nativity, the fioriettini windows worked beautifully, but the linguine thatch had to be propped up by the calamarata donkey.

6. While climbing Mt. Kilimanjaro, which is quite steep up to the very top and then slopes away rather sharply, Rupert constantly had to check his hair dryer for parasites.

7. Wriggling around like that, it took me more than four hours to bury the cat.

8. Deeply offended by the behavior of the counselor whose advice had resulted in a food-fight, a sit-in and an attempted suicide, flinging the rotting pumpkin was almost impossible to resist.

9. Having disproven the existence of dark matter, the Universe suddenly became unexpectedly comprehensible.

10. Without giving it a moment's reflection, seventeen incontinent swallows had been released into the infirmary.

11. Having disproven the existence of dark matter, the Universe became smug and complacent.

Answers

1. Who is perusing? Nobody? Is the car wearing the hat?

2. Who is too full?

3. Who was unable to extract the squid?

4. What ranged in size? I?

5. Who constructed the pasta nativity?

6. No error.

7. What was wriggling? It should be the subject of the following clause but isn't.

8. Who was offended?

9. Who had disproven dark matter?

10. Who had not given it a moment's reflection?

11. In this case, apparently the Universe is who had disproven dark matter. No error.

Adverbs and Adjectives

Adjectives modify nouns. Adverbs modify either verbs or adjectives. These are often confused in common speech. An adjective may modify its noun either by preceding it or by being a predicate nominative that refers back to the subject when a copulative (linking) verb is used:

- *Penelope was indecisive.* "Indecisive" modifies "Penelope". "Be" is a copulative verb.

- *The umpire looked foolish.* "Foolish" modifies "umpire".

A number of verbs can be copulative: be, look, seem, stay, remain, smell, appear.

An adverb modifies a verb or an adjective:

- *The umpire looked foolishly at the underdone turnip.* "Foolishly" is an adverb modifying the verb "looked".

- *The strangely confusing sentence irked the librarian.* "Strangely" is an adverb modifying the adjective "confusing".

Note: While it is true that most adverbs end in "ly" many do not. Also, some lovely adjectives end in "ly" just to be perverse and confusing.

Adverbs and Adjectives Playsheet

Match modifiers with what they modify in the following examples.

1. Aunt Agatha looked cold as she opened her presents.

2. Aunt Agatha looked coldly at Uncle Cuthbert as she opened her parcel containing the infamous holiday assortment of industrial adhesives, one of which had quite handily, in an as yet unexplained case of misidentification, taken second place in the Pixley Festival of Disagreeable Cheeses.

3. Boadicea took refuge behind an enormous decomposing turnip, prominently displayed in the booth representing the Unrepentant Recovering Reductionists.

4. The soft singing seraphim found the stringy otter cheese revolting.

5. The softly singing seraphim found the stringy otter cheese quickly.

6. The bold brazen basilisk spoke with wit and candor of the disadvantages of eating squeaky sweets in the courtroom.

7. The boldly brazen basilisk spoke with wit and candor of the disadvantages of eating sweets squeakily in the courtroom.

8. This daffodil smells sweet and sings sweetly, though it seems only marginally sweeter than Saturday's marginal entries – seemingly.

9. Unable to distinguish Braille E's from I's, the flabbergasted curmudgeon felt bad about feeling so badly.

10. The queen looked beautiful as she looked imperiously at the impudent haddock.

11. The misanthrope looked furtively about, trying avidly not to look furtive.

12. Aunt Agatha had only just recovered from the awful, confusing, but highly memorable funeral.

13. Uncle Cuthbert had been pleasantly surprised and diverted by the awfully confusing funeral.

14. Boadicea agreed that it was hard to picture the intensely unassuming Uncle Aloysius stalking a reindeer, even after his apparent success with the irascible organ-grinder.

Answers

1. Aunt Agatha looked cold. "Cold" is an adjective modifying Aunt Agatha. "Looked" is, in this case, a copulative verb linking Aunt Agatha and "cold".

2. Aunt Agatha looked coldly at Uncle Cuthbert. "Coldly" is an adverb modifying "looked".

3. Boadicea took refuge behind an enormous decomposing turnip, prominently displayed in the booth representing the Unrepentant Recovering Reductionists. "Enormous" and "decomposing" are adjectives that modify "turnip". "Unrepentant" and "recovering" are adjectives that modify "reductionists".

4. The soft singing seraphim found the stringy otter cheese revolting. "Soft" and "singing" are adjectives that modify seraphim. "Stringy" is an adjective that modifies "otter cheese". "Revolting" is an adjective that modifies "otter cheese". "Find" is in this case a copulative verb.

5. The softly singing seraphim found the stringy otter cheese quickly. "Softly" is an adverb that modifies "singing". "Singing" is an adjective that modifies seraphim. "Quickly" is an adverb that modifies "found".

6. The bold brazen basilisk spoke with wit and candor of the disadvantages of eating squeaky sweets in the courtroom. "Bold" and "brazen" are adjectives that modify basilisk. "Squeaky" is an adjective that modifies sweets.

7. The boldly brazen basilisk spoke with wit and candor of the disadvantages of eating sweets squeakily in the courtroom. "boldly" is an adverb that modifies the adjective "brazen". "Brazen" modifies basilisk. "Squeakily" is an adverb that modifies the verb "eating".

8. This daffodil smells sweet and sings sweetly, though it seems only marginally sweeter than Saturday's marginal entries – seemingly. "Sweet" is an adjective that modifies "daffodil". "Sweetly" is an adverb that modifies "sings". "Marginally" is an adverb that modifies "sweeter". "marginal" is an adjective that modifies "entries". "Seemingly" is an adverb modifies "seems".

9. Unable to distinguish Braille E's from I's, the flabbergasted curmudgeon felt bad about feeling so badly. "Flabbergasted" is an adjective that modifies curmudgeon. "bad" is an adjective that modifies "curmudgeon". "Badly" is an adverb that modifies the verb "feeling".

10. The queen looked beautiful as she looked imperiously at the impudent haddock. "Beautiful" is an adjective that modifies "queen". "Imperiously" is an adverb that mod-

ifies the verb "looked". "Impudent" is an adjective that modifies "haddock".

11. The misanthrope looked furtively about, trying avidly not to look furtive. "Furtively" is an adverb that modifies "looked". "Avidly" is an adverb that modifies "trying". "Furtive" is an adjective that modifies "misanthrope".

12. Aunt Agatha had only just recovered from the awful, confusing, but highly memorable funeral. "Only just" is an adverb that modifies the verb "recovered". "Awful" is an adjective that modifies "funeral". "Confusing" is an adjective that modifies "funeral". "Highly" is an adjective that modifies "memorable". "Memorable" is an adjective that modifies "funeral".

13. Uncle Cuthbert had been pleasantly surprised and diverted by the awfully confusing funeral. "Pleasantly" is an adverb that modifies the verb "surprised". "Awfully" is an adverb that modifies the verb "confusing". "Confusing" is an adjective that modifies "funeral".

14. Boadicea agreed that it was hard to picture the intensely unassuming Uncle Aloysius stalking a reindeer, even after his apparent success with the irascible organ-grinder. "Hard" is an adjective that modifies "it". "intensely" is an adverb that modifies "unassuming". "After" is an adverb that modifies the verb "stalking". "Apparent" is an adjective that modifies "success". "Irascible" is an adjective that modifies "organ-grinder".

Projects

1. If you have ever participated in a competition, describe the experience and evaluate the positive/negative effect it had on you and your self-esteem. Take a position on whether competition among young people should be mandatory, encouraged, discouraged, or prohibited. Present arguments and evidence to justify your position.

2. Consider the illegal copying of copyrighted material. Take a position on how illegal it should be and how severe the consequences should be. Does such copying destroy creativity? Which would most effectively maximize a theoretical "universal happiness quotient", complete freedom to copy or the total elimination of copying? Use examples to support your conclusion.

Chapter 11

Vocabulary: The Bat and the Sandwich, Part 2

It would be a **distillation** of many arts. It would be a sandwich! Bucephalus preferred to work on his vision in isolation and started **ferreting** out a **chaotic** and **eccentric** array of raw materials, an apparently **capricious aggregation** which **elicited** bemused **perplexity** in onlookers to whose queries he replied with a **cryptic** "It's a sandwich." Thus **unencumbered** by any constraints (including common sense), prose, verse, and melody were devised. Apricots in **brine**, melons, and pickled haddocks were acquired together with an **incandescent** weasel named Chernobyl. Bucephalus gradually became **cognizant** of the fact that his acquisitions were increasingly chosen for their **inexplicability** and their **efficacy** in foiling speculation by the growing crowd of curious spectators.

The day arrived. By nature not so much **nocturnal** as **crepuscular**, Bucephalus found the transition to spending a few days **diurnally** to be quite comfortable. As his cart descended the hill from the forest, he

distillation n. refinement

ferret v. seek out
chaotic adj. messy
eccentric adj. peculiar
capricious adj. unpredictable
aggregation n. collection
elicit v. bring forth
perplexity n. confusion
cryptic adj. puzzling
encumbered adj. weighed
 down
brine n. salt water
incandescent n. glowing

cognizant adj. aware

inexplicability n. the state
 of being inexplicable, unexplainable
efficacy n. effectiveness

nocturnal adj. active at
 night
crepuscular adj. active at
 twilight
diurnal adj. active during
 the day

found the fair had sprawled all about the countryside. A **spate** of performance art seemed to have taken over as three red squirrels worked on an apparently **anarchic** play, a **travesty** in which each in turn **imitated** a series of world leaders, and a band of voles wielding wooden **cutlasses** and mounted upon an old wooden wagon on which a mast had been erected were rehearsing something superbly **cacophonous** with inspired **vivacity**.

spate n. wave

anarchic adj. opposed to rule
travesty n. satire
imitate v. mimic
cutlass n. curved sword

cacophonous adj. discordant
vivacity n. liveliness

The fairground proper was composed of several **concentric** circles of stalls at the center of which stood a small hill crowned by the **judicial** platform and the panel of judges consisting of a stoat, three turkeys, an ocelot named George, and a parrot with a wooden leg named Monache. As Bucephalus arrived, they were engaged in heated debate over **censorship**, the motives of the body having been **impugned** by a **vociferous pacifist** and **toxophilite** waving a **seditious** banner while a mob of kangaroos shouted him down with accusations of **hypocrisy**.

concentric adj. sharing a center
judicial adj. judging

censorship n. suppression of ideas
impugn v. accuse
vociferous adj. loud
pacifist n. peace lover
toxophilite n. lover of archery
seditious adj. subversive
hypocrisy n. duplicity

The **unassuming** Bucephalus, together with Chernobyl, avoided the **contentious** spectacle, found a spot with sufficient space for their entry, set up their props, utensils, ingredients, tightrope, trapeze, cannon, condiments, and launched into a few **rigorous** last

unassuming adj. modest
contentious adj. quarrelsome

rigorous adj. thorough

minute practice sessions before the judging. When the time came, the most spectacular sculpted sandwich began to take form amid **pirouettes, arias, recitations** and a **poignant pas de deux**. Baffled as to how to rate the performance and the resultant **repast**, the judges, **forsaking** tradition, created a new category, called it "**Eclectic Bombast**" and gave the entry first place in a field of one.

pirouette n. rotation in dance
aria n. solo vocal in opera
recitation n. presentation
poignant adj. moving
pas de deux n. dance for two
repast n. meal
forsake v. abandon
eclectic n. assorted
bombast n. pomposity

Glossary

anarchic adj. Opposed to rule or government; radical, rebellious, chaotic, lawless.

anarchist n. One opposed to government; revolutionary, rebel, radical.   Anarchistic adj.

aggregation n. Collection. Aggregate adj.

aria n. A solo vocal piece with accompaniment as in an opera.

bombast n. Overdone pretentious speech or writing; pomposity, pretentiousness. Bombastic adj.

brine n. Salt water.

cacophonous adj. Jarring, dissonant, inharmonious sounds or music. Cacophony n.

capricious adj. Whimsical and unpredictable; impulsive, erratic. Caprice n. Capriciousness n.

censorship n. Suppression of expressed ideas; expurgation, bowdlerization.   Censor v.

chaotic adj. Messy, disordered, disorganized, entropic, muddled, confused, hectic. Chaos n.

choreograph v. To formulate movement sequences as in dance; design, plan, direct.

cognizant adj. Fully informed, aware, conscious; mindful. Cognizance n.

concentric adj. With or having the same center.   Concentricity n.

contentious adj. Quarrelsome, argumentative, fractious, controversial.

crepuscular adj. Of, related to, or active during dawn and dusk; twilight.

cryptic adj./n. Puzzling, obscure, enigmatic, mysterious.

cutlass n. A short heavy curved sword with nautical connections.

distillation n. Refinement.

diurnal adj. Active during the day.

eccentric adj. Peculiar, odd, weird.   Eccentricity n.
        n. Person with those qualities.

eclectic adj.   Made up of combined elements from diverse sources; assorted, diverse, miscellaneous.
        n. One that follows an eclectic method.

efficacy n. Ability, capacity, competence, effectiveness, efficaciousness, performance, potency. Efficacious adj.

elicit v. Bring forth, obtain, extract, educe. Elicitation n.

encumber v. Weigh down, impede, burden.

ferret [out] v. Dig out, search for.

forsake v. Relinquish, abandon, desert, renounce.

hypocrisy n. Insincerity, duplicity, sanctimony.

imitate v. Emulate, mimic. Imitation n. That which is made as a likeness or copy. Imitative adj. Imitation n.

impugn v. Charge, accuse, censure. Impugnable adj.

incandescent adj. Glowing, radiant, luminous, shining, refulgent. Incandesce v.

inexplicability n. The quality or state of being inexplicable; unexplainable. Inexplicable adj.

intersection n. Junction, crossroads, juncture. Intersect v.

isolation n. Seclusion, separation, segregation. Isolate v.

judicial adj. Legal, judging, court, trial, official, sensible.

nocturnal adj. Active during the night.

orthodox adj. Accepted, traditional, conventional. Orthodoxy n.

pirouette n. A full body rotation on point of toe or ball of foot in ballet.

pacifist n. Peacekeeper, peace lover. Pacifistic adj.

pas de deux n. A dance for two, especially in ballet.

recitation n. Presentation of memorized material in public performance; recital, presentation, performance.

repast n. Meal, banquet, buffet, feast, collation.

rigor n. Rigidity, strictness, firmness, thoroughness, accuracy. Rigorous adj.

rigorous adj. Meticulously accurate; thorough, precise, meticulous, scrupulous. Rigor n.

seditious adj. Of or relating to violent opposition to established authority; subversive, treasonable, rebellious.

spate n. Craze, wave, epidemic.

spectacle n. Vision, sight, show, scene, exhibition. Spectacular adj.

speculate v. Guess, hypothesize, conjecture.

sufficient adj. Adequate, ample, satisfactory.

sufficiency n. An ample or adequate supply.

tedium n. Boredom, monotony, dullness, boredom. Tedious adj.
toxophilite n. One who loves archery.
travesty n. Satire, parody, mockery.
unassuming adj. Modest, humble, unpretentious.
vivacious adj. Lively, energetic, cheerful. Vivacity n.
vivacity n. Exuberance, liveliness, energy, verve. Vivacious adj.
vociferous adj. Characterized by noisy violent outcry; voluble,
    raucous, vocal, strident.

Quiz

1. Bucephalus
    A. worked with the coterie on his entry.
    B. had no common sense.
    C. elicited bemused perplexity in onlookers.
    D. collected a strange array of raw materials.

2. Onlookers asking Bucephalus questions about his project
    A. were told that it was a sandwich.
    B. were chaotic and eccentric.
    C. had no common sense.
    D. questioned his use of unconventional media.

3. Bucephalus
    A. was active during the night.
    B. was active during the day.
    C. was active morning and evenings.
    D. was aquatic and arboreal.

4. The fair had many
    A. entries involving pumpkins.
    B. entries involving performances.
    C. entries from fur bearing carnivores.
    D. entries involving experimental geraniums.

5. Chernobyl
    A. suffered from gout.
    B. devised prose, verse, and melody.
    C. glowed.
    D. was scaly.

6. _____ were in salt water.
    A. Melons   B. Eels
    C. Prose, verse, and melody   D. Apricots

7. Three red squirrels
    A. parodied world leaders.
    B. wielded cutlasses.
    C. invited world leaders.
    D. quoted world leaders.

8. The pacifist
    A. was waving a ridiculous banner.
    B. wielded a cutlass.
    C. was hypocritical.
    D. enjoyed archery.

9. The sandwich took form amid
    A. ranting and raving.
    B. penguins and pangolins.
    C. singing and dancing.
    D. screaming and retching.

10. The show judges
    A. awarded the sandwich "best of show".
    B. considered ballet to be hypocritical.
    C. were baffled as to how to rate the sandwich.
    D. were influenced by the mob of kangaroos.

Answers

1. D.
2. A.
3. C.
4. B.
5. C.

6. D.
7. A.
8. D.
9. C.
10. C.

Language Notes

Metaphors

A metaphor is a language device that invokes an image or concept through a familiar reference that is figuratively but not literally relevant to the subject at hand. (Clearly, metaphors are easier to define through the use of metaphor than by abstract definition.) When you *pop someone's bubble, see the light at the end of the tunnel,* find yourself *up the creek without a paddle, have too many irons in the fire,* or *burn your bridges,* you are using some of the vast wealth of metaphor that has become an established part of English vocabulary. Metaphors are so integrated into our language that we often give little thought to their origin or even to the fact that they are metaphors. When, for example, in a Western or other period film the need for haste is conveyed by telling a character to *"step on it"*, few viewers recognize the anachronism in a nineteenth century character using a twentieth century metaphor inspired by the automobile.

Commonplace metaphors such as these convey meaning clearly and obviously but are so overused that they add little poetry or imagination to the narrative and have become clichés to be avoided. Original metaphors, however, present one of the most fertile corners of the language for the seeds of creativity. Verbs, nouns, adjectives, and adverbs may all be metaphors to add variety, color, and elaborate imagery to a description: "She *wilted dramatically* at the *grating voice* of the *choked* garbage disposal."

Mixed Metaphors

A metaphor becomes mixed when the initial subject of the reference shifts.   Mixed metaphors can be very descriptive and occasionally extremely apt, particularly when used in dialog as a character note.   They do present problems however, frequently distracting the reader from the subject presented to the language used to present it.   One must stop to collect one's thoughts for example, when someone says: *I can see the carrot at the end of the tunnel* or *you can get into hot water skating on thin ice.*   Such utterances cause one's mind's eye to stumble head over heels.   Not to put too fine a point on it, nor to belabor that point, but changing horses in mid metaphor does have the effect of placing a hurdle in the stream of ideas and should be used only when that type of lurching conceptual disorientation is desirable.

> *I think we have misunderestimated the can of worms we threw away with the bathwater.*

> *They're fat cats spinning their web with a tentacle in every pie.*

Similes

The simile is just a metaphor made obvious with the use of "like" or "as".   *His tie was like a comatose basilisk* or Douglas Adams' wonderful inverted simile: *The spaceships hung in the air just like bricks don't.*   Strictly speaking, in formal English "like" should be used when comparing nouns and "as" when comparing verbs.   Thus the simile referring to how objects hang in the air (or don't, as the case may be) should be: *The spaceships hung in the air just as bricks don't,* but here one must defer to Adams who no doubt considered both options before choosing the less formal "like".

Excessive Audible Punctuation – the "Like" Problem

Many teachers and logophiles deplore the rampant usage of the word "like", which, in the speech of some, mostly young, Americans, is sprinkled liberally throughout every sentence. Most dictionaries do not attempt to define this most common usage of the word and to some extent it defies definition. It appears to function as meta-language or possibly as audible punctuation, when indeed it has any function at all, and generally seems intended to draw attention to the following word or phrase as if to say somewhat apologetically: "This may not be just the right way to say this, but here it is." It may precede any part of speech: "He like lurched into the like shed and offered the thespians a like enormous decomposing turnip."

Interestingly, very similar semi-apologetic self-referential language has been in common use for much longer than "like" has, and has also tended to become habitually overused. This expression however, has been largely a shibboleth of the academic elite. I am referring now to the phrase "as it were". Usually regarded as an equivalent to "so to speak", it too draws attention to an expression, which it may either precede or follow, and seems also to convey an apologetic tone. Though seldom used with quite the frequency of the monosyllabic "like", it does dominate the speech of some scholars. "This irksome kerfuffle, as it were, caused great concern among the impatient bureaucrats."

One of the great contemporary artists of the English language, Christopher Hitchens, describes in his *The Other L Word* how he has attempted with some success to combat this use of "like" in his classroom, maintaining that "you have to talk well in order to write well, and you can't write while using 'like' as punctuation." Professor Hitchens himself has been known to use "as it were" from time to time, but, unlike some of his Oxbridge comrades, does so judiciously and in keeping with his own admonition: "A speech idiosyncrasy is really justifiable only if it's employed very sparingly and if the user consciously intends to be using it."

Thus in multiple environments a need for this type of apologetic meta-language exists, and has been met by very different expressions which seem to have established themselves inextricably in our language culture. One interesting approach to the problem might be for those addicted to the use of "like" to try substituting "as it were" and vice versa. The jarring incongruity that would result might not solve the problem at all, but it would certainly make the speakers acutely aware of the verbal habits they have developed.

"Like" Playsheet

Strike out instances of "like" that perform no function.

1. As the like massive diplodocus like pranced over the field like a slug in a like tutu, like three hundred tiny penguins waving like stuffed rabbits and ducks like descended from the like hills like a swarm of malicious like parakeets.

2. The like minded like administrators sat in a like circle on the lawn like surrounded by like a dozen opportunistic spoon wielding like skateboarders like a wagon train beset by befeathered like Pawnees.

3. Like father like son, the like tiny elephant like routed the like putrid like waffle-wielding Ibos like an avenging diminutive leviathan in like 10 minutes of like raucous trumpeting and charging.

4. Though they did like like dinner theater, particularly when it like mimicked recent events in the like play yard, like neither Rowland nor Boadicea like liked the idea of like waving the green sausages about like demented like clockwork monkeys.

5. Traveling like languorously over the like sward like the two dispirited knights they were, the two saw a like enormous waddling bishop with like a flask of like delicious mead and like half a hundredweight of like fish tacos.

6. When like confronted by the like resplendent like garment of which she'd like never like seen the like, and after being like told that like all the like irreverent like rabble like such costumes, she like agreed to appear to like like the outfit, much like she had like agreed to like persuade the lord chancellor to like appear to like picnics in the like swamp.

Answers

1. As the ~~like~~ massive diplodocus ~~like~~ pranced over the field like a slug in a ~~like~~ tutu, ~~like~~ three hundred tiny penguins waving ~~like~~ stuffed rabbits and ducks ~~like~~ descended from the ~~like~~ hills like a swarm of malicious ~~like~~ parakeets.

2. The like minded ~~like~~ administrators sat in a ~~like~~ circle on the lawn ~~like~~ surrounded by ~~like~~ a dozen opportunistic spoon wielding ~~like~~ skateboarders like a wagon train beset by befeathered ~~like~~ Pawnees.

3. Like father like son, the ~~like~~ tiny elephant ~~like~~ routed the ~~like~~ putrid ~~like~~ waffle-wielding Ibos like an avenging diminutive leviathan in ~~like~~ 10 minutes of ~~like~~ raucous trumpeting and charging.

4. Though they did ~~like~~ like dinner theater, particularly when it ~~like~~ mimicked recent events in the ~~like~~ play yard, ~~like~~ neither Rowland nor Boadicea ~~like~~ liked the idea of ~~like~~ waving the green sausages about like demented ~~like~~ clockwork monkeys.

5. Traveling ~~like~~ languorously over the ~~like~~ sward like the two dispirited knights they were, the two saw a ~~like~~ enormous waddling bishop with ~~like~~ a flask of ~~like~~ delicious mead and ~~like~~ half a hundredweight of ~~like~~ fish tacos.

6. When ~~like~~ confronted by the ~~like~~ resplendent ~~like~~ garment of which she'd ~~like~~ never ~~like~~ seen the like, and after being ~~like~~ told that ~~like~~ all the ~~like~~ irreverent ~~like~~ rabble like such costumes, she ~~like~~ agreed to appear to ~~like~~ like the outfit, much like she had ~~like~~ agreed to ~~like~~ persuade the lord chancellor to ~~like~~ appear to like picnics in the ~~like~~ swamp.

Projects

1. Read three pages of a novel, counting the metaphors and similes. Can you find a single page anywhere that contains none? Try rewriting a page to eliminate similes. How does the page sound afterwards? Which is better?

2. Describe imagined entries in the "eclectic bombast" category in a competition <u>using</u> as many misplaced modifiers as you can. Rewrite the piece repairing the modifiers. Example: *Putting the finishing touches on the model-railroad/pumpkin-carving entry, several setbacks involving rhubarb flinging and pig races arose which caused bridges to collapse and trains to derail which displeased the judges.* Corrected: *As the finishing touches were put on the model-railroad/pumpkin-carving entry, several setbacks occurred involving rhubarb-flinging and pig races that caused bridge collapses and derailments which displeased the judges.*

3. Construct or transcribe some common speech which uses the word "like" excessively and gratuitously and substitute "as it were" in each case. How does the result sound to you? Describe the difference in impression that such a speech would inspire.

4. If you are in the habit of using "like" in your speech, spend a day substituting "as it were" and note the difference in reception your words evoke. Describe that difference.

Chapter 12

Vocabulary: The Troll, the Wolf, and the Egg Whisk

Eustace was **elated** at the **accolades** he had received from his co-conspirators after his success in the role of fairy-god-troll, and was **assiduously** seeking further victims of **adversity** upon whom the group could practice their **beneficence**. He stood seven feet tall and was excessively **hirsute**. He had one large eye that **monopolized** the left side of his face, three **superfluous digits** on each paw, and a beard in which you could lose a badger (He knew this from bitter experience). Acutely aware that physical limitations restricted either his roles to **grotesque** creatures or his audience to the exceptionally **gullible**, he was determined to seek out particularly **credulous** recipients for their **altruistic charades** in order to **augment** the scope of his **thespian** prospects.

Deluged by Eustace's queries about other **hapless** inhabitants of the forest, and **conterminous** kingdoms, Sodbury racked his brains for inspiration as he sat under an alder tree in the forest preparing a **sumptuous** feast of nachos laced with prawns, eel, and haddock. The cat mentioned a lass who **spewed** precious jewels

elated adj. delighted
accolade n. praise

assiduous adj. diligent
adversity n. misfortune
beneficence n. kindness
hirsute adj. hairy
monopolize v. dominate
superfluous adj. excess
digit n. finger

grotesque adj. ugly
gullible   adj.   easily
    misled
credulous adj. gullible
altruistic adj. working to
    benefit others
charade n.   make believe
augment v. increase
thespian adj. theatrical
deluge v. flood
hapless adj. unfortunate
conterminous adj. adjacent
sumptuous adj. lavish

spew v. spurt

out of her mouth whenever she talked, which behavior was conveniently **lucrative** in the short term but lost its appeal after a few dinner conversations. Then there was the lad with an **adhesive** goose and the one with a **proboscis** like a cassava melon. None of these seemed to **fadge** well with Eustace's ambitions.

lucrative adj. monetarily rewarding

adhesive adj. sticky
proboscis n. nose

fadge v. suit

"Oh yes", put in the cat suddenly, "There's the young man who wanted to learn what fear was. You could certainly do him a favor just by popping up unexpectedly."

After a few seconds' thought, they both rejected the suggestion speaking **simultaneously** with **disparagement** "**Typecasting**".

simultaneous adj. at the same time
disparagement n. distaste
typecast v. stereotype

At this moment, they spied a girl wearing a scarlet kerchief and carrying a basket and a huge bouquet of flowers. Far from any path, they wondered at her **temerity** wandering thus unaccompanied about the **wildwood**. "This certainly deserves attention", announced the cat packing up the **elaborate** repast into a large **hamper**, "Let's tag along lest some misfortune befall her." It soon became evident that her objective was a small cottage visible through the trees. It was also clear that she would not arrive at it any time soon as she **digressed** from her route to pick every flower she saw. "Gullible enough, do you think?"

temerity n. boldness

wildwood n. unsullied forest
elaborate adj. ornate
hamper n. basket

digress v. wander away from

"Looks very promising", **prognosticated** Eustace as they **sped** toward the cottage in order to reach it before the child. There they found the door ajar and an **emaciated** wolf whining **piteously** as it was being **pummeled** by an elderly lady with a **gargantuan** egg whisk.

"That will be enough of that", demanded the cat, entering the hut **undeterred** by the overwhelming size of the combatants who stopped and stared with wonder at the tiny **overshod** animal. "Now put that thing down", he continued. The lady complied readily as she noticed Eustace

prognosticate v. predict
sped v. past tense of speed
emaciated adj. lean and hungry
piteous adj. arousing pity
pummel v. beat
gargantuan adj. enormous
deter v. discourage

overshod adj. wearing overshoes

enough

squeezing in through the door. Then, turning to the troll, Sodbury **queried,**

query v. to ask a question

"Do you think you can do a wolf emulating a grandmother?" Delighted at the opportunity, Eustace **donned** a nightdress "What's my motivation?"

> don v. to put on (clothing)

"Improvise", responded the cat. Then to the other two "And you two sit quietly over here and behave yourselves" indicating a bench in a dark corner of the room. "Refreshments will be served after the performance."

No sooner were they settled than a knock came at the door. "Come in" bade Eustace in a **deliberately disingenuous falsetto**.

> deliberate adj. intentional
> disingenuous adj. deceitful
> falsetto n. the high voice range

The girl entered the darkened room and, seeing the troll-acting-a-wolf-acting-a-grandmother, remarked "what a big eye you have Grandmother!"

"The better to spot camels with" improvised the beast, desperately seeking inspiration.

"What an awful lot of fingers you have!" she continued, staring at the **extraneous appendages** on his paws.

> extraneous adj. extra
> appendage j. attachment

"The better to calculate in **hexadecimal**" falsettoed the troll with more assurance.

> hexadecimal n. base 16

"What a whopping great beard you have!" exclaimed the lass.

"The better to lose a badger in" responded Eustace after a brief frustrated pause.

The seafood nachos were well received by all (particularly the **ravenous** wolf) following the performance, including an **itinerant** woodcutter who happened by to catch the end and a brief **encore**.

ravenous adj. hungry

itinerant adj. wandering

encore n. repetition

Glossary

accolade n./v. An expression of approval; praise, honor, tribute.
adhesive adj. Having sticky or gluey properties. Adhesive n. something with adhesive properties. Adhere v. To stick.
adversity n. A state of misfortune or ill fate; hardship, difficulty, danger, affliction. Adverse adj.
altruistic adj. Inclined to do works for the benefit of others. Altruism n.
appendage n. Limb, member, adjunct, attachment, accessory.
assiduous n. Diligent, industrious, hard-working, persevering.
augment v. To increase in size; extend, magnify. Augmentation n.
beneficence n. The state of being kind or charitable. Beneficial adj. Benefit v.
charade n. A readily obvious pretense or parody; farce, travesty, make-believe.
conterminous adj. Sharing a common boundary; adjacent, neighboring, contiguous.
credulous adj. Disposed to believe without due consideration; gullible, trusting. Credulity n.
deliberate adj. Intentional, purposeful. v. To think carefully and often slowly.
deluge v. To flood, inundate, overflow. Deluge n. A flood.
deter v. To discourage, daunt, dissuade, prevent. Deterrent n.
digit n. Finger or toe. Also a number.

digress v. To wander from, turn aside, stray from; deviate.
Digression n.

disingenuous adj. Deceitful, insincere, devious, dishonest.

disparagement n. A belittling comparison; deprecation, distaste, opprobrium, derogation. Disparage v.

don v. To put on (clothing), dress in.

elaborate adj. Rich in detail; ornate, complex, intricate.
v. To express in greater detail; to create. Elaboration n.

elated adj. Joyful, glad, ecstatic, jubilant. Elate v. Elation n.

emaciated adj. Thin, withered, gaunt. Emaciation n.

emulate v. To mimic, copy. Emulation n.

encore n. A repetition of part of a musical or dramatic work in response to requests from the audience. From French *encore*, "again".

extraneous adj. Unessential, extra, excess.

fadge v. To suit, match, or be appropriate. To fit with.

falsetto n. The high range of the voice.
v. To speak or sing in a falsetto voice.

gargantuan adj. Enormous, huge, gigantic, massive, vast.

grotesque adj. Bizarre, ugly, gross, monstrous, misshapen. Grotesque n. one that is grotesque. Grotesqueness n.

gullible adj. Easily misled; credulous; susceptible, innocent, trusting. Gullibility n.

hamper n. A large basket with a cover. ,
v. To hinder, obstruct, impede.

hapless adj. Unfortunate, ill fated, luckless, wretched, miserable.

hexadecimal n. The base 16 numbering system, commonly used in conjunction with the binary numbering system and associated devices.

hirsute adj. Hairy.

itinerant adj. Wandering, traveling, peripatetic, nomadic. Itinerate v. To wander. Itinerant n. One who wanders.

lucrative n. Monetarily rewarding. profitable productive.

monopolize v. To dominate by excluding others. Monopoly n.

overshod adj. Wearing overshoes. Adjectival past participle of verb overshoe, to put on or wear an overshoe or Wellington (wellies).

piteous adj. Arousing pity; pathetic, pitiful, wretched. Pity v. Pity n.

proboscis n. Nose, snout, trunk, antenna.

prognosticate v. To foretell, foresee, augur, presage, portend, predict. Prognostication n. Prognosticative adj.

pummel v. Hit, punch, pound, strike, batter.

query v. To ask or question. Query n. A question.

ravenous adj. Extremely hungry; voracious, famished, starving, rapacious.

simultaneous adj. At the same time. Simultaneity n.

sped v. Past tense of verb to speed.

spew v. To spurt, eject, emit.

sumptuous adj. Lavish, luxuriant; extravagant, opulent, spectacular.

superfluous adj. Beyond what is necessary or sufficient; extra, surplus, redundant, excess. Superfluity n.

temerity n. Foolhardy disregard of danger, recklessness, fearlessness, foolhardiness. Temerarious adj.

thespian adj. Of or related to drama and the theater; theatrical. n. One who acts in the theater.

typecast v. To confine to a specific type of role in theater according to type; stereotype, classify.

wildwood n. A forested area in its natural state.

Quiz

1. Eustace was _____ at the response he received after playing fairy-god-troll.
   A. confused
   B. disappointed
   C. excited
   D. delighted

2. Eustace was seeking
   A. people he could help.
   B. victims of gum disease.
   C. victims of sunstroke.
   D. hairy people.

3. Eustace had
    A. hairy toes.
    B. a large eye that was eating the left side of his face.
    C. an unusually large number of fingers.
    D. slippery fingers.

4. Eustace
    A. was happy playing grotesque creatures.
    B. wanted to expand his voice range.
    C. was exceptionally gullible.
    D. wanted to play a variety of roles.

5. Sodbury suggested helping
    A. an irascible cliff-dwelling hermit.
    B. the blue bell fairy of Soggy Bottom.
    C. the wolf.
    D. a boy with a sticky goose.

6. Sodbury
    A. put the meal into a basket.
    B. gave the bluebell fairy an egg whisk.
    C. popped up unexpectedly.
    D. spoke disparagingly of cassava melons.

7. Eustace found the opportunity to play the wolf
    A. unexpected.
    B. challenging.
    C. ludicrous.
    D. ill conceived.

8. Eustace spoke with
    A. the grandmother.
    B. his mouth full.
    C. a disguised high voice.
    D. the bluebell fairy.

9. A badger
  A. had once been lost in Eustace's beard.
  B. was stuck to the goose.
  C. objected to the seafood nachos.
  D. watched the show attentively.

10. The wolf was
  A. deceived by the badger.
  B. lean and hungry.
  C. good at counting in hexadecimal.
  D. itinerant.

Answers

1. D.	6. A.
2. A.	7. B.
3. C.	8. C.
4. D.	9. A.
5. D.	10. B.

Language Notes

Definitions of Good English?

Errors and Non-Errors to Avoid

(Note: the searches used in this study to determine predominant usages in various regions of the web are simply snapshots of an organically changing picture. Numbers will vary and the conclusions drawn may even become refuted by future developments. Also, contexts can be confusing and these searches may well contain spurious, irrelevant and misleading hits, but are nonetheless probably fairly representative on the whole.)

What is correct English? What does it mean to speak and write correctly? There is so much discussion about what is and is not correct, whether dictionaries and texts should prescribe correct usage or simply describe prevailing usage and how obsessed one should be with using language well. The **Reader Rule** – choose a mode of expression suitable to the reader – is clearly the answer to these questions.

Very simply, correct language usage is that which conveys to the intended audience the message and the impression the writer would like to give. It is assumed that students aspiring to produce college-level work will find a fairly formal variety of Standard English (SE) to be most suitable. Other environments may demand very different modes of communication – aboard a Liberian freighter, on an alligator farm, or a pipeline crew, SE could easily be entirely inappropriate, alienating and possibly hazardous.

This preferred SE language standard is associated with educated speakers of the language and, although there exist minor differences between the SE of different regions and countries, in most cases these are minor spelling or pronunciation variations which do not in any way interfere with comprehension of written material from one English speaking country to another. In all important respects, there does exist a universal English standard.

The vast majority of English grammar and style rules are not in dispute (*See* Disputed Aspects of English Grammar p200). Those targeted by standard exams such as the SAT and others are deserving of study and close observance. Although breaking rules may well be an appropriate device to use from time to time for emphasis or effect as has certainly been done extensively for that purpose by many great literary figures, one must always consider what impression such infringements will give one's readers. In general, failure to break a rule rarely results in criticism or gives offense, while the commission of a stylistic or grammatical infraction (real or perceived) may well provide others with a basis for critical judgment. If one does not know one's audience well enough to rule out the possibility of a negative response, it is probably best not to supply grounds for one.

Some common grammar rules are questionable and indeed the arguments for prohibiting some commonly eschewed usages have been convincingly refuted. However, the audience-impression argument is still the clear measure of expressive suitability. If there is a likelihood that a split infinitive, a synesis error, or use of "none" as a plural noun may be perceived as an error (whether or not this perception is nonsense), it is simply better to avoid the usage in question.

Formal Written English

The language targets set by the SAT, ACT and TOEFL exams, among others do agree very closely and establish a firm standard rule set. For academic purposes this differs very little from country to country.

(This excerpt is from an excellent anonymous article which originally appeared in Wikipedia as *Formal Written English*, an entry that has since vanished to be redirected to one entitled Standard English which contains far less information.)

> Formal written English is a version of the language which is almost universally agreed upon by educated English speakers around the world. It takes virtually the same form no matter the local spoken dialect. In spoken English, there are a vast number of differences between dialects, accents, and varieties of slang. In contrast, local variations in the formal written version of the language are quite limited.
>
> Learners of English are in danger of being misled by native speakers who refer to American English, Australian English, British English or other varieties of English. While it is true that many regional differences between the forms of spoken English can be documented, the learner can easily fall into the trap of believing that these are different lan-

guages. They are instead mostly regional variations of the spoken language and such variations occur within these countries as well as between them.

The differences in formal writing that occur in the various parts of the English-speaking world are so slight that many dozens of pages of formal English can be read without the reader coming across any clues as to the origin of the writer, far less any difficulties of comprehension.

A popular American website about errors in English, written by a professor at a west coast U.S. university guiding his students towards preferred constructions of written English, contains almost nothing among its hundreds of entries with which a counterpart thousands of miles away in Sydney or London would disagree. Certainly, disputes about pronunciation and colloquial expressions used in speech abound. But in the written language these are relatively few.

Disputed Aspects of English Grammar

A number of usages have commonly been assumed to be mistakes, but some of these assumptions have come to be either discredited or largely ignored in everyday and even scholarly use.

The Synesis Error
There is one specific usage that the SAT exam clearly considers to be a mistake but which abounds on the web as well as in scholarly writings. This is the "synesis" error which is given special treatment here because it is a case in which adhering to overwhelmingly accepted usage will nonetheless cost points on a test.

Here is a sample SAT question from the collegeboard.com site (official home of the SAT) in which the student is expected to identify the error in the sentence by it's A,B,C,D,E letter designation:

*After**A** hours of futile debate, the committee*
*has decided to postpone**B** further discussion*
*of the resolution**C** until their**D** next meeting.*
*No error**E***

Correct Answer: D

Explanation given:

- The error in this sentence occurs at (D). A pronoun must agree in number (singular or plural) with the noun to which it refers. Here, the plural pronoun "their" incorrectly refers to the singular noun "committee".
- The sentence may be corrected as follows: After hours of futile debate, the committee has decided to postpone further discussion of the resolution until its next meeting.

This is an example of synesis which is defined as "A construction in which a form, such as a pronoun, differs in number but agrees in meaning with the word governing it, as in *If the group becomes too large, we can split them in two.*"

Indeed, there does exist a mismatch in this sentence, but it must also be noted that the crime of synesis occurs consistently in the speech and writing of academics as well as global web writing. This is very probably because alternatives are even worse.

The above example uses a collective noun, *committee*, and the synesis error involves referring to it with the plural *their* while the SAT suggested solution involves using the singular *its* instead. Collective nouns are, however, often used in the plural, particularly in the UK. *The herd of wildebeest came over the parking lot waving their tails.* The solution suggested by the College Board above doesn't really solve the problem at all – suppose the committee entered the boardroom and took their seats. It makes no sense to say that the committee took its seat.

A more difficult question arises when there is a singular noun, not a collective noun: *Everyone should have **their** pencil handy.* This is clearly a more serious synesis mismatch because the question of the collective noun does not even arise; *everyone* is irrefutably singular and *their* is plural. However, this choice may still not be quite as egregious as the alternatives: *Everyone should have **his** pencil handy* (sexist) or *Everyone should have **his or her** pencil handy* (irksomely awkward). The problem is that there is no non-gender-specific singular pronoun to use and the plural *they* is uncomfortably substituted. This synesis error has become largely accepted and is to be found in profusion throughout academia and the web.

Hit frequency on the whole web:
everyone should have their 18,200,000
everyone should have his 5,800,000
everyone should have his or her 1,930,000

Hit frequency in UK academic sites (site:ac.uk):
everyone should have their 78,100
everyone should have his 5
everyone should have his or her 3

Hit frequency in US and other universities(site:.edu):
everyone should have their 413,000
everyone should have his 125,000
everyone should have his or her 8
Of course it is perfectly possible that the above search counts might include irrelevant hits such as:
May I introduce Mr. Monk. **Everyone should have his** *book handy* or *May I introduce Mr. and Mrs. Flanagan.* **Everyone should have their** *book handy.* But it is hoped that these perfectly ac-

ceptable sentences will occur with similar frequency and cancel out.

Given the choice of sexism, awkwardness and the synesis error, the dominant choice of the English speaking world is synesis.

Other commonly condemned usages are:

- Splitting an infinitive. *To boldly go where no man has gone before.*
- Ending a sentence with a preposition. *That is the sort of nonsense I will not put up with.*
- Using "none" as a plural noun. *None of them were quite ready to be displayed in the curling club locker room.*
- The use of "who" as the object of a verb or preposition where "whom" is correct. *Who did the provost direct to remove the badger from the auditorium? Who did you receive the holiday collection of industrial adhesives from?*
- A pronoun in the objective case after a comparative with "than" or "as" (sometimes called an elliptical reference): *He is even more scrofulous than me. She is just as revolting as him.*

Each of these prohibitions has been disputed and common usage has rendered them largely moot, but does this mean that it is safe to use these rejected forms? The only good answer to this is the ultimate one: the Reader Rule. There are without doubt many people, academics among them, who are firmly convinced that synesis, split infinitives and the rest of these are indeed incorrect. If one's readers or audience might contain some of these, and offending them is undesirable, is it not advisable to avoid the use of constructs that are, by many, perceived as wrong? Nobody will censure a writer for not splitting an infinitive when given the opportunity, and using "whom" correctly when most of the world doesn't, will convey a more academic impression.

Hit count on the whole web:
"by whom" 2,720,000
"by who" 15,200,000

UK academic sites (site:ac.uk/):
"by whom" 141,000
"by who" 37,200

USA universities (site:.edu):
"by whom" 809,000
"by who" 196,000

University of California Los Angeles (site:ucla.edu)
"by whom" 1,410
"by who" 343

While "Whom" users are undeniably outnumbered on the web as a whole by more than 5:1, they dominate in education by about the same ratio. The use of "whom" correctly tends to define the speaker as educated. It's incorrect use could easily appear pretentious and ignorant however. When in doubt as to which of "who" or "whom" is correct, use "who" (or better yet, read the chapter and learn when to use which. See Who and Whom P 147.)

Similarly, the use of a subject pronoun after "than" is rare, even among academics and would probably raise eyebrows: *Hermione is much more confused than I. The cafeteria staff couldn't possibly fling the cat further than he.*

Which Language to Choose

Clearly in order to make a favorable impression upon a learned audience, standard grammatical usage is best. Complex combined constructs and challenging vocabulary may be appropriate, but above all, make sure to resolve all references correctly and keep coordination constructs parallel and logical. To add a particularly academic flavor, use "whom" and elliptical references correctly.

On the other hand of course, if the intent is to offend, horrify and shock one's audience, one is advised to resort to other dialects beyond the scope of the current volume.

Our Strange Language

Many words have very specific meanings according to the context in which they are used. Even terms listed as synonyms, for example *vision* and *sight*, can take on very different meanings. For example, a man telling his wife/girlfriend that she looks a vision is quite different than telling her that she looks a sight.

An idiom is an expression whose meaning cannot be gleaned from the individual words. English is rich in idioms. Many are so much a part of the language that native speakers do not really think of them as idioms yet they can be very confusing to students of English who must attempt to understand by examining the literal meaning of the words. How can one guess the meaning of phrases like *to win hands down, to make a clean breast of,* or *to go in for?* Far more confusing are those idioms that twist and reverse their meanings:

When the stars are out, they are shining. When a light is out, it is not.

A *wise man* and a *wise guy* do not mean the same thing.

Your house may *overlook* the ocean, which means you see the ocean from there. However, if you *overlooked* the ocean, it means you didn't see it.

Winding up starts a toy but ends a speech.

We spell two words exactly the same but pronounce them differently without even thinking about it: You *tear* along the dotted line but have a *tear* in your eye.

Today you *read* the biography of Rupert the Spleenless, but yesterday you *read* an account of the flatulent hermit of Pixley.

Horse, and *worse* look like they rhyme but don't, nor do
      lord and *word*
      beard and *heard*
      vague and *ague*
      break and *bleak*
      steak and *streak*
      tortoise and *turquoise*
      wallet and *mallet*
      low and *now.*

However, these differently spelled words do rhyme:
      busy and *dizzy*
      gauge and *age*
      bury and *very*
      low and *toe.*

Projects

1. Rewrite The Bat and the Sandwich with synonyms.

2. How many strange idioms can you think of, and how many can you weave into the same sentence?

3. Write an essay in support of or opposition to the implementation of a standard of consistency between spelling and pronunciation in English.

4. Listen to the speech of a parent or teacher. How many grammatical errors can you pick out? Try transcribing dialog from an interview. Can you find any examples that contain no errors?

Epilogue

Traditional and Nontraditional Writing Classes

Writing can be an utterly jubilant activity, but a significant level of creative ecstasy is rarely experienced by high school-aged students and is very nearly impossible to achieve in the traditional school environment.

Experience in most high school classrooms (using the mass-production educational model and presided over by often well-meaning but uninspired pedants) so often prompts students to conclude that essay writing is always something decidedly distasteful. The essay, however, can be an eye-opening opportunity for endless creativity and variation, whose flexibility and expressive potential is limited only by the writer's ability to weave cogent content into a dazzling fabric of felicitous diction – well, perhaps it needn't always go that far, but the point stands: essay writing is what one makes of it and the more one does, the better one gets and the easier and more enjoyable it becomes. This is the philosophy that the writing classes that gave birth to this work espouse and implement.

A Different Approach to the Acquisition of Writing Skills

It is very hard to generate enthusiasm for writing when one's labor results only in an ephemeral entity whose sole purpose for existence is to be the subject of a cursory critical evaluation and a sin-

gle mark in a grade book. Essay writing is often much more excit-
ing and interesting when one is writing for an audience and not
just for a teacher who will glance over the paper quickly, make a
few red marks, and return it. Unfortunately, few alternatives to
uninspired and anemic instructional mediocrity exist, though some
are emerging. The online and hybrid writing class for homeschoolers which inspired this book is but one example. A very
different learning environment exists when students have the opportunity to write for an audience – for the class as a whole, the
teacher, and ultimately, after some honing and revision, for a larger audience of fellow students and parents and for the public in
web and print media. Students also have impressive and persuasive material to put in their portfolios and resumes.

A class grade in an accredited high school is certainly of some
value, but it becomes somewhat feeble when placed next to a port-
folio of published works whose message and mastery are directly
evident to the observer. Such a tangible record of student
achievement is far more compelling than a simple letter on a piece
of paper reflecting a perfunctory perusal and a possibly skewed
evaluation by an only marginally interested and probably harried
and preoccupied instructor.

One Example of an Alternative to the Traditional Classroom

For nearly ten years, our College Preparatory English class has
been held largely online, with all handouts and assignment submission taking place in an online classroom, but with a weekly
traditional classroom meeting concurrently available online, free
to auditors, and recorded for review, in which corrected papers,
grammar, writing style, and the language of great writers and
speakers is presented, analyzed and discussed. Now with full online application sharing, together with full audio and video, online
students may participate equally with classroom students.

Many traditional and online grammar and writing resources are at best uninspired and at worst, misleading and error ridden. We feel that polished formal standard English should dominate in the classroom in both written and spoken examples, for emulation is one of the most powerful pedagogical devices and it is a crime to use it to propagate errors and misusages. At the same time, there is no reason for grammar and writing study to be dry and boring. Our class uses the one-room schoolhouse paradigm with students of multiple ages and abilities working and studying together.

- Correct and sophisticated language study
- Writing with a purpose and for an audience
- Writing for personal enjoyment

For more information on studying writing online, or for help in setting up an alternative study program   see http://abacus-es.com/cpep/resources.html

Appendix A

Glossary

a cappella adj. adv. Sung without instrumental accompaniment.

abbreviate v. Shorten, abridge, reduce, truncate, curtail.
    Abbreviated adj. Abbreviation n.

abjure v. Recant, renounce, eschew, repudiate, reject, forswear, retract, disown. Abjuration n.

abrogate v. To abolish, repeal, revoke, rescind, annul, retract.
    Abrogation n.

abstinence n. Act of refraining from. Abstain [from] v.
    Abstemious adj.

abundance [of] n. Profusion, plenty, wealth. Abundant adj.

accolade n. An expression of approval; praise, honor, tribute.

accretion n. Augmentation by gradual external addition. Growth, increase, addition, expansion, supplementation, proliferation, accumulation, enlargement, increment, waxing.
    Accretionary, accretive adj.

acerbity n. Sourness of character, appearance, or tone; acidity, acrimony, asperity, astringency, tartness. Acerbic adj.

ad hoc adj. Devised for a single purpose. Improvisatory, extemporaneous, impromptu, unrehearsed.

adhesive adj. Having sticky or gluey properties. Adhesive n. something with adhesive properties. Adhere v. To stick.

adulate v. To praise or admire excessively; fawn on, flatter, elevate, worship. Adulatory adj. Adulation n.

adulation n. High praise; adoration, worship, admiration.
    Adulate v. Adulatory adj.

adversity n. A state of misfortune or ill fate; hardship, difficulty, danger, affliction. Adverse adj.

advocate [for] v. To speak, plead, or argue in support of. Recommend, endorse, champion, propose, favor, defend, promote, urge, advise, justify, campaign for, commend, espouse, countenance. Advocate n. Advocation n. Advocative adj.

aesthetic adj. Pertaining to beauty; artistic. Aesthetic n.

aggregation n. Collection. Aggregate adj.

agitate v. Disturb, excite, perturb, trouble, disconcert. Agitation n. Agitated adj.

agoraphobia n. Fear of open spaces. Agoraphobic adj.

alacrity adj. Speed; enthusiasm, readiness, promptness, rapidity.

altruistic adj. Inclined to do works for the benefit of others. Altruism n.

ambivalence n. Uncertainty or indecisiveness about which of multiple courses to follow; indecision, dubiety, ambiguity. Ambivalent adj.

amicable adj. Agreeable; friendly, good-natured, harmonious. Amicability n.

anachronism n. An instance of someone existing or an event occurring in other than proper chronological, historical sequence. A time anomaly.

anachronistic adj. Out-of-place in time. Anachronism n.

anarchic adj. Opposed to rule or government; radical, rebellious, chaotic, lawless.

anarchist n. One opposed to government; revolutionary, rebel, radical. Anarchistic adj.

ancillary adj. Supplemental, of secondary importance. Having the characteristics of an added item, such as a workbook provided to support a textbook. Supplementary, additional, subsidiary, accessory, subordinate, auxiliary, contributory. Ancillary n.

anecdote n. Short account of event; story, tale, yarn. Anecdotal adj.

anonymous adj. Nameless, unidentified, unknown. Anonymity n.

anosmia n. The inability to smell or sense odors. Anosmic adj.

antagonist n. Opponent, adversary. Antagonistic adj.

anticipate v. To feel or realize in advance; expect, foresee, predict, await. Anticipatory adj.

apathetic adj. Unconcerned, indifferent; listless. Apathy n.

appellation n. Name, title, designation. Term, address, cognomen, moniker, nickname, description, epithet, sobriquet.

appendage n. Limb, addition, attachment, adjunct, member, accessory.

apprise v. To inform [of]. To notify. make aware, tell, warn, advise, inform, communicate, notify, acquaint, give notice.

approbation. n. Commendation, approval, recognition, praise. Approbatory adj.

apt adj. Precisely suitable, appropriate, fitting, felicitous.

aquatic adj. Of or pertaining to water or the sea; marine.

arboreal adj. Of, pertaining to, or living in a tree or trees; sylvan.

ardor n. Fiery intensity, passion, zeal, avidity, sedulity.

aria n. A solo vocal piece with accompaniment as in an opera.

aspirant n. One who aspires; candidate, applicant, contender.

aspire v. To have a great ambition or goal; seek, aim, hope, wish. Aspirant n.

assiduous n. Diligent, industrious, hard-working, persevering.

astute adj. Observant, keen, perceptive, perspicacious, shrewd, incisive. Astuteness n.

atavistic adj. Characteristic of a throwback. Of or relating to reversion to a former or more primitive state. Regressive. Atavism n.

atrophy n. v. A wasting away through lack of use. To wither or shrink. Atrophic adn. Waste away, waste, shrink, diminish, deteriorate, decay, dwindle, wither, wilt, shrivel.

audacious adj. Foolhardy, daring, brave, bold, impudent, risky. Audacity n.

audacity n. Boldness, daring, fearlessness, impudence, nerve, courage, overconfidence, foolhardiness. Audacious adj.

augment v. To make something greater, larger, or more extensive; enlarge, expand, enhance, magnify. Augmentation n.

aversion [to] n. Dislike for; loathing [of], distaste [for], hatred [of]. Averse adj.

ban n. v. A prohibition. To prohibit. Prohibition, block, restriction, veto, boycott, embargo, injunction, censorship, taboo, suppression, stoppage, disqualification, interdiction, interdict, proscription, disallowance.

banter n. v. Repartee, wit, chitchat, mockery, teasing, persiflage.

bellicose adj. Warlike, belligerent, pugnacious, combative, confrontational, Bellicosity adj.

bemoan v. To express grief over; lament, bewail, regret, mourn.

beneficence n. The state of being kind or charitable.
    Beneficial adj. Benefit v.

benevolent adj. Friendly, helpful, kind, caring, benign.
    Benevolence n.

bibliophile n. One who loves books. Bibliophilic adj.

bombast n. Overdone pretentious speech or writing; pomposity, pretentiousness. Bombastic adj.

brine n. Salt water.

broach v. To bring up [a subject] for discussion or consideration; mention, raise.

Brobdingnagian adj. Immense, enormous, gigantic, huge, vast.

budgie n. A budgerigar, parakeet.

cacophonous adj. Jarring, dissonant, discordant, inharmonious sounds or music. Cacophony n.

cadent adj. Having cadence or rhythm; regularly repetitive.
    Cadence n.

cadre n. A core of competent individuals around whom a larger (often revolutionary) body can form.

camaraderie   n. Trust among friends; amity, solidarity, comradeship.

canonical. adj. Conforming to orthodox or widely-accepted regulations or guidelines.

capricious adj. Whimsical and unpredictable; impulsive, erratic.
    Caprice n. Capriciousness n.

caribou n. A reindeer.

cavalcade n. A procession of horses.

censorship n. Suppression of expressed ideas; expurgation, bowdlerization. Censor v.

censure v./n. To criticize harshly; reprimand, reproach, condemn, remonstrate.

chandler n. One who makes and sells candles.

chandlery n. Candle wares or wares sold by a chandler.

chaotic adj. Messy, disordered, disorganized, entropic, muddled, confused, hectic. Chaos n.

charade n. A readily obvious pretense or parody; farce, travesty, make-believe.

choreograph v. To formulate movement sequences as in dance; design, plan, direct.

chromatic adj. Abounding in color; colorful. Chromaticism n.

chronological adj. Sequential, ordered as in a timeline. Chronology n.

chronology n. A time line or time-ordered sequence. Chronological adj.

circuitous adj. Indirect, roundabout, meandering, winding. Circuity n.

cognizant [of] adj. Aware [of], conscious [of], vigilant, mindful [of]. Cognizance n.

collaborate v. To work together; join forces. Collaborative adj. Collaboration n.

compassion n. Sympathy, mercy, empathy, concern, consideration. Compassionate adj.

compassionate adj. Sympathetic, empathetic, concerned, kindly.

compromise v./n. To settle differences; to cooperate, to concede. Compromising adj.

concentric adj. With or having the same center. Concentricity n.

condescend [to] v. To descend to the level of another; stoop, deign, patronize. Condescension n.

condescending adj. Patronizing, disdainful, haughty, arrogant.

confection n. A sweet preparation such as candy.

confer v. To discuss. To engage in conference. Conference n.

confer v. To give, to bestow upon; award, present, grant. Conferment n. Conferrable adj.

configuration [of] n. Arrangement of parts or elements; relationship. Configure v.

conformist n. Follower of customs; traditionalist. Conform v. Conformity n.

congregation n. An assembly of persons or things; collection, company, flock, group, assemblage, crowd, host.
Congregate v.

conjure (up) v. Call up; invoke, summon.

conscientious adj. Governed by the dictates of conscience; principled. Conscientiously adv. Conscientiousness n.

conspicuous adj. Evident, visible, easy to notice, obvious, clear, apparent, manifest, noticeable, blatant, discernible, salient, perceptible.

constabulary n. A police force. The officers in a police force collectively as a group. Gendarmerie. Constable n.

contentious adj. Quarrelsome, argumentative, fractious, controversial.

conterminous adj. Sharing a common boundary; adjacent, neighboring, contiguous.

contingent [upon, on] adj. Dependent upon events or outcomes not yet determined; dependent [upon, on], conditional, subject [to], reliant [on, upon].

controversy n. A dispute between parties holding opposing views; disagreement, debate. Controversial adj.

convene v. To assemble, to meet as a group; summon, call together.

conventional adj. In accordance with general consensus or practice; predictable. Convention n.

convoluted adj. Having numerous overlapping folds; Intricate, complicated, elaborate complex.
Convolution n. Convolute v.

coprolite n. Fossilized excrement.

coterie n. A small, often select, group of persons who meet frequently for a purpose; click, assemblage.

couch [as] v. Formulate an utterance; express, phrase, imply.

cranium n. The part of the scull enclosing the brain; head, braincase.

credulous adj. Disposed to believe without due consideration; gullible, trusting. Credulity n.

crepuscular adj. Of, related to, or active during dawn and dusk; twilight.

criterion n. A standard of judgment; decisive factor, principle, measure, condition, reason. Plural: criteria

croon v./n. To hum or sing softly; chant, drone.

cryptic adj. Puzzling, obscure, enigmatic, mysterious.

culinary adj. Of or relating to the art of food preparation; cooking, cookery, gustatory.

curcubita n. The genus to which pumpkins belong. Curcurbitic and curcubitive are adjectival forms of curcubita.

cutlass n. A short heavy curved sword with nautical connections.

cynosure n. That which serves as a source of attention, admiration and influence. A guide. Counseling, guidance, counsel, direction. Cynosural. adj.

daunt v. To curtail the courage of, discourage, dismay, deter, dispirit, dishearten. Daunting adj.

dearth n. Scarcity, paucity, exiguity, lack, shortage, insufficiency, deficiency.

debacle n. Fiasco, catastrophe, disaster, shambles, tragedy, calamity.

decry v. Condemn, criticize, disparage, belittle, deprecate, vilipend.

defer [to] v. To yield out of respect or consideration of another's wishes, age or authority; postpone, suspend.
Deferrable adj.

deference n. adj. Courteous respect for the opinion, wishes, or judgment of another. Respect, regard, consideration, honor, esteem, courtesy, homage, reverence, politeness, civility, veneration, thoughtfulness. Deferential. adj. Showing deference.

deleterious [to] adj. Harmful, destructive, inimical, detrimental.

deliberate adj. Intentional, purposeful.
v. To think carefully and often slowly.

deluge v. To flood, inundate, overflow. Deluge n. A flood.

demeaning adj. Belittling, humiliating, degrading, debasing, derogatory. Demean v.

demur n. Objection, protest.

denizen n. Inhabitant, resident, citizen, native.

deprecate v. To belittle; to minimize; to undervalue, disparage, denigrate, derogate, detract, decry.
  Deprecatory adj. Deprecation n.
deprecation n. Expression of disapproval; condemnation, contempt, scorn, disparagement, opprobrium.
  Deprecate v. Deprecatory adj.
deride v. To ridicule; scoff, disparage, disdain.
  Derision n. Derisive adj.
desiccate v. Dry, dehydrate, parch. Desiccated adj.
desiccated adj. Dried out; shriveled, dehydrated, shrunken.
  Desiccate v.
deter [from] v. To discourage, daunt, dissuade, prevent.
  Deterrent n.
detract. v. detraction n.
detractor n. Defamer, libeler, critic, slanderer, disparager, traducer, vilifier.
detriment n. Harm, damage, disadvantage disparagement.
  Detrimental adj.
devoid [of] adj. Lacking, missing, wanting.
diatribe n. A bitter, excoriating denunciation. Tirade, abuse, criticism, reviling, harangue, invective, vituperation, pejorative.
didactic adj. Intended for instruction; educational, instructive, edifying. Didacticism n.
didgeridoo or didjeridu n. A musical instrument of the Australian Aborigines consisting of a long hollow tree limb or bamboo stalk that makes a deep drone when blown into.
digit n. Finger or toe. Also a number.
digress [from] v. To wander from, turn aside, stray from; deviate.
  Digression n.
dilettante n. A dabbler pursuing superficially or amateurishly a few or many arts or fields of knowledge. Dilettantish adj.
  Dilettantism n.
diligent adj. Hard-working; industrious, assiduous, meticulous, conscientious. Diligence n.
diplodocus n. A large herbivorous Jurassic-Epoch dinosaur of the Sauropod suborder.

disavow v. To disclaim responsibility for; deny, renounce, disown. Disavowal n.

disceptation n. Controversy, argument, contention, altercation, argumentation.

discord n. Tension or strife resulting from a lack of agreement; dissension, disagreement, conflict, friction.
Discordant adj.

disdain v./n. To regard with scorn, derision, disparagement, contempt. Disdainful adj.

disheveled adj. Tousled, unkempt, untidy. Dishevelment n.

disingenuous adj. Deceitful, insincere, devious, dishonest.

disintegration [pf] n. Loss of cohesion or unity. Reduction to pieces, fragments. Decomposition, fragmentation, decay.
Disintegrate v.

disorient v. To cause to be disoriented, confused.

disoriented adj. Confused, unsettled, bewildered, perplexed, baffled.

disparagement n. A show of disrespect, contempt, criticism, ridicule, condemnation, scorn, depreciation, disdain, denunciation, derision, denigration, derogation. Disparage v.

disparate adj. Of differing kind, having dissimilar properties; contrasting, distinct, divergent, inconsistent, unequivalent.

distillation n. Refinement.

diurnal adj. Active during the day.

diverge [from] v. Differ [from], deviate [from], depart [from], disagree [with].

divergent adj. Variant, moving apart, differing, deviating, contrary. Diverge v.

diversion n. The act of turning aside from ones path or a distracting entertainment; distraction, amusement, recreation.
Diversionary adj.

don v. To put on (clothing), dress in.

draconian adj. Exceedingly strict, harsh or severe. Hard, stern, drastic, stringent, pitiless.

dumbfound v. To cause astonishment and perplexity; astonish, amaze, astound, stagger, confound, confuse, baffle, bewilder, flummox.

duplicity n. Double-dealing; deceit, deception, disloyalty.
Duplicitous adj.

durable adj. Capable of withstanding wear and tear. Resistant to decay or erosion. Lasting, strong, tough, sound, substantial, reliable, sturdy. Durability n.

eccentric adj. Peculiar, odd, weird. Eccentricity n.

eclectic adj. Made up of combined elements from diverse sources; assorted, diverse, miscellaneous.

ecstatic adj. Delighted, overjoyed, thrilled, elated, rapturous, euphoric. Ecstasy n.

cdifice n. Structure, construction.

edifice n. A building, especially one of imposing appearance or size. An elaborate conceptual structure. Building, house, structure, construction. edificial

educe v. Bring forth; elicit, conclude, evoke, obtain.

efficacy n. Ability, capacity, competence, effectiveness, efficaciousness, performance, potency. Efficacious adj.

effigy n. Image, figure, carving, model, statue, sculpture.

effluvium n. A noxious or ill-smelling exhalation from decaying or putrefying matter. Effluvial adj.

egregious adj. Conspicuously bad or offensive.

egregious adv. Conspicuously bad or objectionable. appalling, dreadful, shocking, notorious, horrific, outrageous, infamous, intolerable, monstrous, scandalous, frightful, heinous, abhorrent, insufferable.

elaborate adj. Rich in detail; ornate, complex, intricate.
v. To express in greater detail; to create. Elaboration n.

elated adj. Joyful, glad, ecstatic, jubilant. Elate v. Elation n.

elicit v. Bring forth, obtain, extract, educe. Elicitation n.

emaciated adj. Extremely thin, undernourished. Skeletal, weak, lean, pinched, gaunt, atrophied, scrawny, attenuate, half-starved, cadaverous, macilent, withered. Emaciate v. Emaciation n

emulate v. To mimic, copy. Emulation n.

enamor v. To inspire with love. [*To be enamored of* is *to be in love with*] encore n. A repetition of part of a musical or dramatic work in response to requests from the audience. From French *encore*, "again".

encumber v. Weigh down, impede, burden.

endemic adj. Peculiar to some specified country or people; prevalent. Endemism n.

enticement n. That which attracts by inspiring hope or desire. Bait, temptation, lure, allure, seduction, inducement, cajolery. Entice v.

envious adj. Feeling, expressing or characterized by envy; covetous, desirous.

envy n. Jealousy, covetousness. Envious adj.

eohippus n. Hyracotherium. The earliest known horse species which lived about 50 million years ago during the early Eocene Epoch (Long after the Jurassic period).

epithet n. A (commonly deprecatory) term used to characterize a person or thing. A label, name, title, description, tag, nickname, designation, appellation, sobriquet, moniker. Epithetic adj.

equivocation n. A statement open to multiple interpretations and often intended to mislead. Ambiguity, casuistry, sophistry, chicanery, speciousness, sophism. Equivocate v. Equivocal adj.

erroneous adj. In error, false, mistaken. incorrect, wrong, flawed, fallacious, faulty, inaccurate, untrue, invalid, unfounded, spurious, amiss, unsound.

evade v. To escape or avoid; dodge, skirt. Evasive adj. Evasion n.

evanescent adj. Short-lived; transient, impermanent, ephemeral.

eviscerate v. Disembowel, gut. Take away a vital or essential part of. Devitalize.

exasperation n. Irritation, frustration, annoyance, vexation. Exasperate n. Exasperated adj.

exemplary adj. Outstanding, excellent, commendable, typical. Exemplify v.

exorbitant adj. Exceeding all bounds. Flagrant, excessive, unreasonable, excessive, extravagant, immoderate.

extol v. Admire, praise, exalt. Extolment n.

extortionate adj. Exorbitant, gouging, excessively expensive, usurious, outrageous, steep, unconscionable, immoderate. Extort v. Extortion n.

extraneous adj. Unessential, extra, excess.

fabricate v. To make, build or construct. Manufacture, form, fashion, shape, frame, assemble, erect.

fadge v. To suit, match, or be appropriate. To fit with.

falsetto n. The high range of the voice.
v. To speak or sing in a falsetto voice.

fardel n. A pack, bundle or burden. Encumbrance, onus, load.

fatuity n. Foolishness, stupidity, absurdity, folly. Fatuous adj.

fatuous adj. Completely or inanely foolish.

fecund adj. Fertile, prolific, fruitful, nubile.

ferret [out] v. Dig out, search for.

fervor n. Hot, intense emotion. Arousal, excitement, zeal, enthusiasm, ardor, passion. Fervid adj.

fester v. To undergo decay, esp. in a wound; inflame, infect, corrupt, irritate, aggravate.

fetid adj. Unpleasant smelling; foul, putrid, rank, fusty. Fetidity n.

flatulent adj. Affected with gasses generated in the bowels. Suffering from wind. Flatus n.

forbear v. Hold back, abstain, refrain from.

forgo v. Abstain from; give up, relinquish, decline.

forsake v. Relinquish, abandon, desert, renounce.

fortuitous adj. Lucky, accidental, chance, unexpected. Fortuity n.

fortuity n. A chance occurrence or event. Coincidence, happenstance. Fortuitous adj.

gall v. Irritate, provoke, infuriate.

garb n. Clothing, dress, attire, costume.

gargantuan adj. Enormous, huge, gigantic, massive, vast.

garish adj. Brash, bright, loud, dazzling, tasteless, gaudy.

gaudy adj. Garish, flashy, kitschy, extravagant, loud, colorful.

genealogy n. Familial ancestry, pedigree, descent, lineage.
Genealogical adj.

genre n. A category, kind, type, sort, variety, genus.

interstitial adj. Occupying the space in between other things, objects or events. Interstice n. A small opening between things.

intrepid adj. Fearless, adventurous, brave, courageous. Intrepidity n.

intrinsic adj. Of or relating to the essential nature of a thing. Inherent. native, built-in, underlying, congenital, inborn, inbred.

intuitive adj. Instinctive, natural, untutored, innate, instinctive. Intuition n. Intuit v

invigilation n. Proctoring [an examination]. Surveillance, superintendence, supervising, supervision, oversight. Invigilate v.

irascible adj. Easily provoked to anger; irritable, fractious, petulant, querulous. Irascibility n.

irrefragable adj. Impossible to refute or controvert, incontrovertible, indisputable, undeniable, irrefutable. Irrefragability n.

irreverence n. Lack of reverence or due respect. Desecration, profanation, sacrilege, blasphemy.

isolation n. Seclusion, separation, segregation. Isolate v.

itinerant adj. Wandering, traveling, peripatetic, nomadic. Itinerate v. To wander. Itinerant n. one who wanders.

jubilation n. Joy, exultation, elation, euphoria, delight. Jubilant adj. Jubilate v.

judicial adj. Legal, judging, court, trial, official, sensible.

Jurassic adj. Of or relating to the geologic period from about 208 to 144 million years ago.

Kant Proper noun. German philosopher who sought to synthesize rationalism and empiricism.

knurly adj. Full of knots; hard; tough. Knurl n.

lachrymose adj. Tearful, crying, weepy, sobbing. Lachrymate v. Lachrymation n. Lachrimation n.

laden adj. Weighed down with a load, loaded, encumbered, burdened. Hampered, weighted, full, taxed, oppressed, fraught. Load v.

laudation n. Praise, approval, acclaim, applause, tribute, ovation, accolade, panegyric, eulogy, commendation, approbation, acclamation, encomium, plaudit. Laud v.

libertarian adj. Tolerant, permissive, broadminded.

lucrative n. Monetarily rewarding. profitable productive.

ludicrous adj. Ridiculous, absurd, preposterous, foolish, comical.

Maasai or Masai Proper noun. An East-African people of Kenya and Tanzania.

mandate n. v. Command, order. Dictate, prescribe, order. Mandatory adj.

matriculation n. The process of being admitted into a group, especially a college or university. Admission, admittance. Matriculate v.

medicate v. To treat with medicine; dose. Medication n.

medication n. Medicine, drug, prescription.

melee n. A confused battle; brawl, clash, fracas, fray, tussle.

miasma n. A noxious or poisonous atmosphere or influence; murk, pall. Miasmic adj. Miasmal adj. Miasmatic adj.

militant adj. Of combative or confrontational nature. Inimical, acrimonious, rancorous, refractory, contumacious, aggressive, warring, fighting, belligerent. Militance, militancy n.

misanthropic adj. Characterized by hatred of humans; unfriendly, antisocial, hostile, malevolent. Misanthrope n.

monopolize v. To dominate by excluding others. Monopoly n.

motley adj. Consisting of an incongruous mixture of types or colors; assorted, miscellaneous, diverse, varied, dissimilar.

mundane adj. Ordinary, common, routine, everyday, commonplace. Mundanity n.

muse n. A source of inspiration. Any of the nine daughters of Mnemosyne and Zeus, each of whom presided over and inspired a different art or science. The muses are Calliope, Clio, Erato, Euterpe, Melpomene, Polyhymnia, Terpsichore, Thalia, and Urania.

nocturnal adj. Active during the night.

nonce n. [for the nonce] The present or particular occasion. [For the] present. [For the] time being.

nonchalant adj. Calm, casual, offhand, relaxed. Nonchalance n.

nostalgia n. A fond longing for things of the past; reminiscence, wistfulness, longing. Nostalgic adj.

nubile adj. Of marriageable age or condition. Nubility n.

obfuscation n. The act of rendering something confusing and in-comprehensible. Evasiveness, deception, equivocation, prevarication, sophistry, obliqueness, sophism.

obsolescent adj. Out of date. Vestigial.

onerous adj. Troublesome or oppressive, distasteful, burdensome, trying, hard, taxing, demanding, difficult, heavy, crushing, exhausting, troublesome, oppressive, laborious, irksome, backbreaking, exigent.

opera n. Plural of opus, a work. A dramatic work incorporating music and singing.

opportune adj. Suited or right in space and time; fitting, appropri-ate, favorable. Opportunity n. Opportunistic adj.

opportunistic adj. Taking immediate advantage of opportunities.

opprobrious adj. Expressing contemptuous disdain or reproach. Scornful, abusive, belittling, disdainful, contemptuous, disparaging. Opprobrium. n.

opulence n. Wealth, lavishness, luxury, magnificence. Opulent adj.

opulent adj. Wealthy; lavish, luxurious, magnificent, sumptuous, affluent. Opulence n.

opus n. An artistic creation; composition, work, piece. Pl. opera

orator n. Speaker, lecturer, narrator. Orate v. Oration n.

ordure n. Excrement, dung. Ordurous adj.

ornate adj. Elaborately, extensively ornamented; complex, high-ly wrought, complicated, flamboyant.

orthodox adj. Accepted, traditional, conventional. Orthodoxy n.

ostentation n. Showiness, affectation, flamboyance, pretension. Ostentatious adj.

ostentatious adj. Displaying wealth; pretentious, showy, boastful, affected, grandiose, flamboyant. Ostentation n.

overshod adj. Wearing overshoes. Adjectival past participle of verb overshoe, to put on or wear an overshoe or Welling-ton (wellies).

owl castings n. Indigestible remnants of an animal devoured whole by an owl and later regurgitated.

pacifist n. Peacekeeper, peace lover. Pacifistic adj.

panacea n. A remedy or medicine proposed for or professing to cure all diseases; cure-all, solution.

pandemonium n. A fiendish or riotous uproar; chaos, bedlam, uproar.

pantomime n. Storytelling without words, using only bodily movements, gestures, and facial expressions. Pantomimic adj. Pantomimist n.

papier-mache n. A combination of paper pulp and glue which can be sculpted or molded.

papyrus n. The writing-paper of the ancient Egyptians, and later of the Romans.

paradox n. A statement or doctrine seemingly in contradiction to the received belief; contradiction, inconsistency, irony. Paradoxical adj.

parental adj. Of or relating to parenthood. Parent n.

parody v. To render ludicrous by imitating the language of; caricature, satire, spoof.

parsimonious adj. Excessively sparing in the use or expenditure of money; thrifty, frugal, miserly. Parsimony n.

pas de deux. A dance for two, especially in ballet.

patriarch n. The chief of a tribe or race who rules by paternal right. Patriarchal adj.

patronymic adj./n. Formed after one's father's name. A name formed after one's father's name.

paucity Scarcity, lack, shortage, insufficiency, deficiency, exiguity.

pecuniary adj. Consisting of or related to money; financial, fiscal, economic.

pedant n. A scholar who makes needless and inappropriate display of his learning; sophist. Pedantic adj. Pedantry n.

pedantic adj. Doctrinaire, sophistic, finicky, arcane.

penchant [for] n. Inclination [to, for], proclivity [for, to], affinity [for, to], predilection [for], fondness [for].

pendulous adj. Hanging, swinging, depending, drooping.

penitence n. Sorrow for a sin with desire to amend and to atone; contrition, repentance, remorse. Penitent adj.

penury n. Indigence, poverty, destitution. Penurious adj.

prudent adj. Wise, careful, cautious, sensible, discreet, wise. Prudence n.

puerile adj. Childish, juvenile, immature, callow.

pugnacious adj. Quarrelsome, confrontational, belligerent, truculent, contentious. Pugnacity n.

pullulative adj. Tending to to breed or increase in number rapidly or abundantly. Swarming, teeming, seething. Pullulate v. Pullulation n.

pummel v. Hit, punch, pound, strike, batter.

purport v. To have the intention of doing; profess, purpose.

purported adj. Presumed to be, supposed.

putrescent adj. Undergoing decomposition of animal or vegetable matter accompanied by fetid odors; rotting, decomposing. Putrescence n. Putrefy v.

querulous adj. Irritable, cantankerous, difficult, petulant, irascible.

query v. To ask or question. Query n. A question.

raconteur n. Storyteller.

raiment n. Garb, clothing, costume.

rancorous adj. Hateful, resentful, ruthless, vengeful, fractious. Rancor n.

raptly adv. Attentively.

ravenous adj. Extremely hungry; voracious, famished, starving, rapacious.

rebarbative adj. Irritating, repellent, annoying, harassing, harrying.

reciprocal adj. Reflecting mutual action or relationship. An equal exchange or substitution. Quid pro quo. Exchange, interchange, tit for tat, equivalent, compensation, substitution.

recitation n. Presentation of memorized material in public performance; recital, presentation, performance.

reclusive adj. Withdrawn, hermit-like; solitary, unsociable, secluded. Recluse n.

reconciliation (with) n. Agreement after a quarrel. Reconcile v.

redolent [of] adj. Having a strong odor; aromatic, fragrant, malodorous, stinking, smelly. Redolence n.

reductionist n. One who attempts to explain a complex set of facts or phenomena by another, simpler set of component parts. Reductionism n.

refulgent adj. Shining radiantly; gleaming, glowing, luminous, radiant. Refulgence n.

refute v. To prove to be wrong; disprove, controvert, contest, deny, counter. Refutation n.

regale v. Amuse, delight, divert, entertain. Regalement n.

relish n./v. Like, delight in, enjoy.

remedial adj. Healing or providing remedy. Treating or overcoming deficiencies. Therapeutic, salubrious, healing, curing, curative, health-promoting, alleviative, salutary, corrective.

remonstrate v. Protest, object, reprove, complain. Remonstrance n. Remonstration n. Remonstrative adj.

remonstration n. objection, protest, complaint, disagreement, dissent, remonstrance, remonstration. Remonstrate v.

repast n. Meal, banquet, buffet, feast, collation.

replica n. A copy or reproduction; imitation, model, facsimile, duplication. Replicate v.

repudiate v. To refuse to have anything to do with; reject, cast off, disclaim, disavow, renounce. Repudiation n.

repudiation n. The act of repudiating.

requisite adj. Necessary, obligatory, mandatory, essential.

rescind v. Abolish, withdraw, annul, cancel, repeal, overturn. Rescindable adj. Rescindment n.

residue n. Remains, dregs, remainder. Residual adj.

resilience n. The ability to recover quickly; pliability, flexibility, toughness, spirit. Resilient adj.

resilient adj. Quick to recover; flexible, tough, durable. Resilience n.

resplendent adj. Magnificent, brilliant, glorious, dazzling, stunning. Resplendence n.

restrained adj. Controlled, restricted, reserved, calm, undemonstrative. Restrain v.

revelry n. Enthusiastic merrymaking; festivities, celebrations, partying. Revelrous adj.

rigid adj. Incapable of or resistant to bending; inflexible, stiff, firm, unyielding. Rigidity n. Rigidify v.

rigor n. Rigidity, strictness, firmness, thoroughness, accuracy.

rigorous adj. Meticulously accurate; thorough, precise, meticulous, scrupulous.

sacrosanctity n. Quality of being sacred or sacrosanct.

sagacious adj. Able to discern and distinguish with wise perception; wise, sage, perceptive, erudite. Sagacity n.

salutary adj. Health inducing; beneficial, helpful, salubrious, constructive.

sardonic adj. Scornfully or bitterly sarcastic; scornful, mocking, derisive, satirical. Sardonicism n.

satire n. parody, mockery, caricature, spoof (informal), travesty, lampoon, skit. Satirical adj. Satirist n.

scatology n. The scientific study of feces. The chemical analysis of excrement (for medical diagnosis or for paleontological purposes). Scatological adj. Of or relating to excrement or its study.

scrutinize v. to observe carefully;   inspect, examine, analyze. Scrutiny n.

seditious adj. Of or relating to violent opposition to established authority; subversive, treasonable, rebellious.

seditious adj. Rebellions against the authority of a state. Inciting public disorder, revolutionary. Rabble-rousing, treasonous, subversive, disloyal. Sedition n.

senile adj. Characteristic of old age. Geriatric, doddering, doting, in one's dotage, decrepit, faltering. Senility n.

serene adj. Unaffected by disturbance; calm, unruffled, tranquil, peaceful, unruffled. Serenity n.

simultaneous adj. At the same time. Simultaneity n.

sobriquet n. An affectionate or humorous nickname or assumed name. Appellation, appellative, designation, denomination.

somnolence n. Sleep, sleepiness, drowsiness. Somnolent adj.

sonorous adj. Resounding, resonant, booming, echoing, reverberating.

spate n. Craze, wave, epidemic.

specious adj. Baseless, erroneous, unfounded, false.
    Speciousness n. Speciosity n.

spectacle n. Vision, sight, show, scene, exhibition.
    Spectacular adj.

speculate v. Guess, hypothesize, conjecture.

sped v. Past tense of verb to speed.

spew v. To spurt, eject, emit.

spontaneous adj. Arising from inherent qualities or tendencies without external cause; unprompted, unplanned, impulsive. Spontaneity n.

spurious adj. False, bogus, fake, counterfeit, imitation, unauthentic.

spurtle n. A round wooden stirring utensil for porridge.

squalid adj. Dirty and wretched; filthy foul nasty fetid. Squalor n.

squamous adj. Scaly. Squamulose.

squamulose adj. Covered with small scales; scaly, squamous.

stagnate v. To be or become stagnant. Characterized by lack of motion or vitality. Inaction, inactiveness, inactivity. Stagnant adj.

stereotype n. An example of stereotyping.

stereotype v. Pigeonhole, typecast, categorize. Stereotypic adj. Stereotypical adj.

stigma n. A sign or mark of ignominy, disgrace or infamy. disgrace, shame, dishonor, stain, blot, reproach. Stigmal adj.

stolid adj. Dull, emotionless, unresponsive. Stolidity n.

subsequent [to] adj. Following; succeeding, ensuing, successive, consequent, after.

substantiate v. To verify, confirm, validate, authenticate, prove. Substantiation n.

subvert v. To destroy completely; ruin, undermine, threaten, destabilize. Subversion n. Subversive adj.

succumb [to] v. To cease to resist; yield, submit, surrender.

sufficiency n. An ample or adequate supply. Sufficient adj.

sufficient adj. Adequate, ample, satisfactory. Sufficiency n.

sumptuous adj. Characterized by splendor, suggesting great expense, lavish, luxuriant, resplendent, opulent, extravagant, spectacular.

sundry adj. Various, mixed, miscellaneous.

superannuated adj. Outmoded, obsolete.

venerable adj. Respectable due to age; respected, revered, honored, admired. Venerate v.

verisimilitude n. The quality of appearing to be true or real. Verisimilitudinous adj.

vestigial adj. Of or relating to a remaining or lingering trace of something previously present. Residual, lingering, enduring, remaining. Vestige n.

vindicate v. To clear from blame; support, prove correct.

virtual adj. Existing in effect but not in actual fact; effective, practical, essential. Virtuality n.

visage n. Face, lineament, appearance, likeness, countenance, aspect.

viscosity n. Resistance (in a liquid) to flowing; thickness, stickiness, glueyness, tackiness. Viscous adj.

vivacious adj. Lively, energetic, cheerful. Vivacity n.

vivacity n. Exuberance, liveliness, energy, verve.

vociferous adj. Characterized by noisy violent outcry; voluble, raucous, vocal, strident.

wary (of) adj. Watchful, alert, reticent, concerned, troubled.

wildwood n. A forested area in its natural state.

Appendix B

Parts of Speech

Nouns

Nouns represent a person, place or thing, including abstractions. *Nelson Mandela, book, compost, humor, confusion, exasperation* are nouns. There are a potentially infinite number of nouns as new ones are being invented all the time. English nouns are inflected (changed in form or declined) only to show plural and possessive qualities. "Book" becomes "books" in plural and "book's" would indicate possession as in "the book's jacket".

Only proper nouns, the name of a place, person, day of week, month of year, are capitalized: *Ferdinand, Severus, Rupert, Sir Thomas Crapper, Tuesday, November*, etc.

Pronouns

Pronouns take the place of nouns. There are only a few of these and you already know them all. Who (whom in object case), what, which, that, each, are examples of general pronouns. Apart from *who*, whose object form is *whom* and possessive is *whose*, only the personal pronouns are declined extensively. Declension is used to indicate subject, object, or possessive case according to how they are used in the sentence and depending upon the number, person, and gender of the noun represented by the pronoun. Here is a chart.

Personal Pronoun Declension

number	person	gender*	Cases of Personal Pronouns				possessive adjectives
			subject	object	possessive	reflexive	
Singular	1st	m/f	I	me	mine	myself	my
	2nd	m/f	you	you	yours	yourself	your
	3rd	m	he	him	his	himself	his
		f	she	her	hers	herself	her
		n	it	it	its	itself	its
plural	1st	m/f	we	us	ours	ourselves	our
	2nd	m/f	you	you	yours	yourselves	your
	3rd	m/f/n	they	them	theirs	themselves	their

* m=masculine f=feminine n=neuter

Prepositions

Prepositions represent relationships, either spatial or abstract, between objects. There are only about 50 prepositions and you already know them all. Here is a fairly complete list: *aboard, about, above, across, after, against, along, amid, among, anti, around, as, at, before, behind, below, beneath, beside, besides, between, beyond, by, despite, down, during, except, excepting, excluding, following, for, from, in, inside, into, like, near, of, off, on, onto, opposite, outside, over, past, per, plus, round, save, since, than, through, to, toward, towards, under, underneath, unlike, until, up, upon, versus, via, with, within, without.*

Prepositions may take objects just as verbs may have objects.

The tie hung on him much as a comatose basilisk would.

One cannot say *the tie hung on he.*

Wrong:	Correct:
over I	*over me*
from she	*from her*
for who	*for whom*
of they	*of them*

Verbs
Verb Conjugation Rules

Verbs are inflected (verbs are said to be *conjugated* while nouns and pronouns are *declined*.) to reflect how they are used. Apart from the irregular ones whose unpredictable principle parts, P1, P4, and P5 must be memorized and are listed below, conjugation follows this simple set of rules. New irregular verbs are no longer being created in English so the list of irregular verbs to be learnt is not getting any larger.

Definitions:

vowels : ['a', 'e', 'I', 'o', 'u', 'y']. A vowel will be indicated in context with a capital V.

consonants : all others. Consonants will be indicated in context with a capital C.

doubling characters : ['b', 'd', 'f', 'g', 'l', 'm', 'n', 'p', 'r', 's', 't', 'z'].

The verb "be" is a special case and is ignored in these rules in simple present and past.

All one-syllable verbs have a stressed last syllable.

P1: The verb stem.

P2: Third person singular present indicative.
1. Special case: "have" becomes "has"
2. Modal verb (can, could, will, would, may, might, shall, should, must): remains the same as verb stem
3. Verb ends with Cs or Cz, add "es"
4. Verb ends with Vs or Vz, double the last character and add "es"
5. Verb ends with Cy, drop "y" and add "ies" try → tries, fly → flies
6. Verb ends with "ch", "sh", "x", or "o", add "es" box → boxes, search → searches, wish → wishes go → goes
7. If none of the above, add "s"

P3: present participle.
1. Verb ends with Ce or "ue" (and is not the verb "be"), drop the "e" and add "ing" race → racing, make → making
2. Verb ends with stressed syllable, ending with a single vowel or quV followed by a doubling character: double the last character, and add "ing" rub → rubbing, infer → inferring, quit → quitting
3. Verb ends with "ie", drop the "ie" and add "ying" lie → lying, vie → vying
4. If none of the above, just add "ing"

P4: simple past.
1. If verb is irregular, use past tense make → made, run → ran
2. If verb ends with "e" then drop the "e" and add "ed" grate → grated, date → dated
3. If verb ends with Cy, drop the "y" and add "ied" deny → denied
4. If last syllable is stressed, and ends with a single vowel or quV followed by a doubling character, double the last character and add "ed" rub → rubbed, quip → quipped
5. If none of the above, just add "ed"

P5: past participle.
1. If verb is irregular, use past participle.
2. Otherwise use the same rules as are required for P4.

Irregular Verb List

P1, P4, P5
be, were, been
bear, bore, borne
beat, beat, beaten
begin, began, begun
bend, bent, bent
bid, bade, bidden
bind, bound, bound
bite, bit, bitten

P1, P4, P5
bleed, bled, bled
blow, blew, blown
break, broke, broken
breed, bred, bred
bring, brought, brought
build, built, built
burn, burnt, burnt
burst, burst, burst

P1, P4, P5

buy, bought, bought
cast, cast, cast
catch, caught, caught
chide, chid, chid
choose, chose, chosen
cling, clung, clung
clothe, clad, clad
come, came, come
cost, cost, cost
creep, crept, crept
cut, cut, cut
deal, dealt, dealt
dig, dug, dug
do, did, done
draw, drew, drawn
dream, dreamt, dreamt
drink, drank, drunk
drive, drove, driven
eat, ate, eaten
fall, fell, fallen
feed, fed, fed
feel, felt, felt
fight, fought, fought
find, found, found
flee, fled, fled
fling, flung, flung
fly, flew, flown
freeze, froze, frozen
get, got, gotten
give, gave, given
go, went, gone
grind, ground, ground
grow, grew, grown
hang, hung, hung
have, had, had
hear, heard, heard

P1, P4, P5

hide, hid, hidden
hit, hit, hit
hold, held, held
hurt, hurt, hurt
keep, kept, kept
know, knew, known
lay, laid, laid
lead, led, led
leap, leapt, leapt
learn, learnt, learnt
leave, left, left
lend, lent, lent
let, let, let
lie, lay, lain
lose, lost, lost
make, made, made
mean, meant, meant
meet, met, met
pay, paid, paid
plead, pled, pleaded
put, put, put
read, read, read
ride, rode, ridden
ring, rang, rung
rise, rose, risen
run, ran, run
sake, sook, saken*
say, said, said
see, saw, seen
seek, sought, sought
sell, sold, sold
send, sent, sent
set, set, set
sew, sewed, sewn
shake, shook, shaken
shear, sheared, shorn

P1, P4, P5

shine, shone, shone
shit, shat, shat
shoe, shod, shod
shoot, shot, shot
show, showed, shown
shrink, shrank, shrunk
shrive, shrove, shriven
shut, shut, shut
sing, sang, sung
sink, sank, sunk
sit, sat, sat
sleep, slept, slept
slide, slid, slid
slink, slunk, slunk
smell, smelt, smelt
speak, spoke, spoken
spend, spent, spent
spit, spat, spat
split, split, split
spread, spread, spread
spring, sprang, sprung
stand, stood, stood
steal, stole, stolen
stick, stuck, stuck
sting, stung, stung

P1, P4, P5

stink, stank, stunk
stride, strode, strode
strike, struck, struck
strive, strove, striven
swear, swore, sworn
sweep, swept, swept
swim, swam, swum
swing, swung, swung
take, took, taken
teach, taught, taught
tear, tore, torn
tell, told, told
think, thought, thought
throw, threw, thrown
thrust, thrust, thrust
tread, trod, trodden
wake, woke, woken
wear, wore, worn
weep, wept, wept
win, won, won
wind, wound, wound
work, wrought, wrought
wreak, wrought, wrought
wring, wrung, wrung
write, wrote, written

* used only with prefix

Prefixes Used with Irregular Verbs

mis, par, un, under, over, be, for, fore, out, in

Verb Forms

		Principle parts (to be learnt for irregular verbs)				Predictable forms
		P1	P4	P5	P3	P2
	infinitive	base	simple	past participle	present participle	simple present, 3rd person singular
regular	(to) work	work	worked	worked	working	works
irregular	(to) sing	Sing	Sang	Sung	Singing	Sings
	(to) make	Make	Made	Made	Making	Makes
	(to) cut	cut	cut	cut	cutting	cuts
	(to) do	Do	Did	Done	Doing	Does
	(to) have	have	had	had	having	has
	infinitive	base	past simple	past participle	present participle	present simple
	(to) be	be	was, were	been	being	am, are, is

Rules for Creating Verb Phrases in Perfect, Progressive, and Passive

These rules, originally used in an algorithmic English language computer program, are easy for a machine to implement or for a human who understands machines. Two simple tools are used to make them generally comprehensible: the verb box, and the phrase line. The verb box contains the verb to be treated and the phrase line is used to hold the complete verb phrase as it accumulates a part at a time from right to left. We start by putting the main verb into the verb box.

Verb box:

| SEE |

Phrase line:

| |

There are four steps in the process to be learnt in order 1-4 covering simple present and future, perfect, progressive, and passive respectively. However, when the steps are applied, the most recent one learnt is applied first i.e. rule four first, then three, then two, and one.

(Note that phrases using modal verbs (may, might, shall, should, can, could, must) are all handled exactly as the verb 'will' is below, substituting the modal verb for 'will.')

Step 1: SIMPLE PRESENT, PAST AND FUTURE (MODAL)

Verb in verb box: go   phrase line becomes:

Present:	(pronoun) [P1 or P2 of verb in box]	I go (he goes)
Past:	(pronoun) [P4 of verb in box]	I went
Future:	(pronoun) will [P1 of verb in box]	I will go

Verb in verb box: see phrase line becomes:

Present:	(pronoun) [P1 or P2 of verb in box]	I see (he sees)
Past:	(pronoun) [P4 of verb in box]	I saw
Future:	(pronoun) will [P1 of verb in box]	I will see

Step 2: PERFECT

If phrase is not in perfect: go to step 1.
If phrase is perfect:

1. Take verb from the verb box, change it to its P5 (past participle) form and put it to the right of the phrase line (there may be other verbs already there, put it in front of them)
2. Put the verb "have" into the verb box.
3. Go to step 1.

Step 3: PROGRESSIVE

If phrase is not progressive: go to step 2.
If phrase is progressive:
1. Take verb from the verb box, change it to its P3 (present participle) form and put it to the right of the phrase line (there may be another verb already there, place the new one in front of it.)
2. Put the verb "be" into the verb box.
3. Go to step 2.

Step 4: PASSIVE

If phrase is not passive: go to step 3.
If phrase is passive:
1. Take verb from the verb box, change it to its P5 (past participle) from and put it to the right of the phrase line.
2. Put the verb "be" into the verb box.
3. Go to step 3.

For Example.   PASSIVE PROGRESSIVE PERFECT FUTURE with the verb SEE: put verb in verb box and start with empty phrase line.

Verb box:

SEE

Phrase line:

Step 4, passive. It is passive, so take P5 of the verb in the verb in the verb box (SEE), put it at the end of the phrase line and put BE into the verb box:

Verb box:

BE

Phrase line:

→ SEEN

Step 3, progressive. It is progressive, so take P3 of the verb in the verb box (BE), put it at the end of the phrase line (before what is already there) and put BE into the verb box:

Verb box:

BE

Phrase line:

→ ‚BEING SEEN

Step 2, perfect. It is perfect, so take P5 of the verb in the verb box (BE), put it at the end of the phrase line (before what is already there) and put HAVE into the verb box:

Verb box:

HAVE

Phrase line:

→ BEEN BEING SEEN

Step 1, simple present, past, and future. It is future, so conjugate the verb in the verb box in simple future: (pronoun) WILL HAVE, and put it in the phrase line in front of what is already there:

Verb box:

HAVE

Phrase line:

→ HE WILL HAVE BEEN BEING SEEN

For Example. PROGRESSIVE PERFECT with the verb DO: put verb in verb box and start with empty phrase line.

Verb box:

DO

Phrase line:

Step 4, passive. It is not passive, so go to step 3.

Step 3, progressive. It is progressive, so take P3 of the verb in the verb box (DO), put it at the end of the phrase line (before what is already there) and put BE into the verb box:

Verb box:

BE

Phrase line:

→ DOING

Step 2, perfect. It is perfect, so take P5 of the verb in the verb box (BE), put it at the end of the phrase line (before what is already there) and put HAVE into the verb box:

Verb box:

HAVE

Phrase line:

→ BEEN DOING

Step 1, simple present, past, and future. It is future, so conjugate the verb in the verb box in simple future: (pronoun) WILL HAVE, and put it in the phrase line in front of what is already there:

Verb box:

HAVE

Phrase line:

→ SHE HAS BEEN DOING

For Example.   PASSIVE PROGRESSIVE with the verb find: put verb in verb box and start with empty phrase line.

Verb box:

FIND

Phrase line:

Step 4, passive. It is passive, so take P5 of the verb in the verb in the verb box (FIND), put it at the end of the phrase line and put BE into the verb box:

Verb box:

BE

Phrase line:

→ FOUND

Step 3, progressive. It is progressive, so take P3 of the verb in the verb box (BE), put it at the end of the phrase line (before what is already there) and put BE into the verb box:

Verb box:

BE

Phrase line:

	→ BEING FOUND

Step 2, perfect. It is not perfect, so go to step 1.

Step 1, simple present, past, and future. Conjugate the verb in the verb box (pronoun) BE (SHE IS), and put it in the phrase line in front of what is already there:

Verb box:

BE

Phrase line:

	→ SHE IS BEING FOUND

Adjectives

Adjectives modify nouns. *Small, black, knobby, impossible, peculiar, sticky, reprehensible* are adjectives. There are a potentially infinite number of adjectives. Adjectives are normally used in their positive forms but may be inflected into comparative and superlative forms to indicate degree in relation to other objects. Some two-syllable adjectives and all adjectives with more than two syllables use more to form the comparative and most to form the superlative forms.

positive	comparative	superlative
tall	taller	tallest
grumpy	grumpier	grumpiest
indecisive	more indecisive	most indecisive

A few adjectives have irregular comparative and superlative forms:

positive	comparative	superlative
good	better	best
bad	worse	worst

Adverbs

Adverbs modify verbs, adjectives, or other adverbs. Most adverbs end in "ly" and most adjectives may be made into adverbs by adding "ly". *Unwillingly, remotely, quickly, pointlessly* are adverbs. There are as many adverbs as there are adjectives.

Conjunctions

Conjunctions are words that connect other words, phrases, and clauses. Coordinating conjunctions, those which link independent elements, are: *and, but, or, nor, for, yet, and so*. A subordinating conjunction joins a subordinate (dependent) clause to a main (independent) clause. *After, although, as, because, before, how, since, than, that, though, if, once, till, until, when, where, whether,* and *while* are subordinating conjunctions.

Articles

Articles There are only three of them. They identify nouns and may either be indefinite, *a* or *an* depending on whether the noun that follows starts with a vowel sound, or definite. The definite article, *the,* is used when a certain specific object is referred to by the noun, otherwise the indefinite article is used. Normally an article is required for a singular noun, though there are many exceptions. (*See* Articles p48).

Interjections

Interjections may be injected anywhere in speech or writing with no regard for grammar, placement, propriety, or common sense. *Oh, wow,* and *alas, ouch, hey, d'oh* are examples, as are oaths, curses, expletives, and most profane blurtings.

Appendix C

Fundamental Greek and Latin Roots

ROOT	SAMPLE WORD	*MEANING*
a-, an-, without	• achromatic, • amoral, • atypical, • anaerobic	• colorless • unethical • uncharacteristic • not needing oxygen
-able, -ible forms adjectives and means "capable or worthy of"	• likable, • flexible	• friendly • bendable
-acious tending to	• audacious • bodacious	• daring • remarkable prodigious
acro- topmost, at the tip	• acrobat • acrophobia	• trapeze artist, gymnast • fear of heights
agog- leader	• demagogue	• false leader of people
agri- field	• agrarian • agriculture	• of or relating to farming • cultivation of fields

ROOT	SAMPLE WORD	*MEANING*
ambi- both	• ambidextrous	• skilled w/both hands
ante- before	• antecedent • ante-nuptial • antebellum	• preceding event or word • before the wedding • before the Civil War
anthro- man	• anthropology • misanthrope • philanthropy	• study of man • recluse (hater of mankind) • love of mankind: charity
-anthrop-, human	• misanthrope • philanthropy •anthropomorphic	• One who hates humankind • One who loves humankind • having human form
anti-, ant-, opposite; opposing	• anticrime • antipollution • antacid	• opposed to crime • opposed to pollution, • opposed to acid
aqua- water	• aquaduct • aquatic	• *passageway for water* • *living in water*

ROOT	SAMPLE WORD	*MEANING*
arch- chief, first	• archetype • archbishop • archeology	• *original model* • *chief bishop* • *study of antiquities*
arch- government, ruler	• monarch	• *sole ruler*
-ation forms nouns from verbs	• creation • civilization	• that which is created • that which is civilized
auto-, self, same	• autobiography • automobile • autopilot	• biography of its author • moves under its own power • that which steers itself
bio-, bi-, life, living organism; biology, biological	• biology, • biophysics • biotechnology • biopsy	• the study of life • application of physics to life • application of technology to life • sample of living tissue

ROOT	SAMPLE WORD	*MEANING*
-chron-, time	• anachronism • chronic • chronicle • synchronize • chronometer	• *something out of time sequence* • *occurring over time* • *a historic record by time* • *to match in time* • *device to measure time*
chronos- time	• chronology • anachronism • chronicle	• timetable of events • something out of time sequence • to register events in order
cid, cis- to cut, to kill	• incision • homicide • fratricide	• to cut (surgical) • killing of a man • killing of a brother
clam- to cry out	• clamorous • acclamation	• loud • shouted approval
co-, together	• coauthor • coedit • coheir	• collaborating author • edit in collaboration • one who inherits with others

ROOT	SAMPLE WORD	*MEANING*
cognit-, to learn	• cognition • incognito • agnostic	• knowledge • unknown or un recognized • lacking know-ledge/skeptical
com- with, to-gether	• combine • commerce • communicate	• merge with • trade with • convey informa-tion (with anoth-er)
corpor-, body	• incorporate • corporeal • corpse	• organize into a body • pertaining to the body • a dead body
cred- to believe	• credence • credulity • incredulous	• belief • belief with no facts • not believing, skeptical
de- away, off; generally in-dicates rever-sal or remov-al in English	• deactivate • debone • defrost • decompress • deplane	• make inactive • remove bones • remove frost • uncompress • disembark from a plane

ROOT	SAMPLE WORD	*MEANING*
-dem- people	• democracy • demography • endemic • pandemic	• government by the people • measurement of people • peculiar to a specific people • affecting many or all people
-dict-, to say	• contradict • dictate • diction • edict • predict	• speak against • say aloud, pronounce • clarity of speech • pronouncement • to say previously
dis- not, not any	• disbelief • discomfort • discredit • disrepair • disrespect	• lack of belief • lack of comfort • shame, bring to disrepute • not in proper repair • showing a lack of respect
-duc-, to lead, bring, take	• deduce • produce • reduce	• draw from, conclude from • bring forth • bring back, retract

ROOT	SAMPLE WORD	*MEANING*
-fy, -ify forms verbs and means "to make or cause to become"	• purify • acidify • humidify	• make pure • make more acid • make more damp
geo- Earth; geography	• geography, • eomagnetism • geophysics • geopolitics	• study of the earth • magnetism of the earth • physics of the earth • politics of the earth
-gram, something written or drawn, a record	• cardiogram • telegram	• record of the heart • transmitted record
-graph, something written or drawn; an instrument for writing, drawing, or recording	• monograph • phonograph • seismograph	• a writing on a specific subject • a record of sound • a device for producing an earthquake record
-gress- to walk	• digress • progress • transgress	• to walk off the path, wander • to walk forward • to walk across, misbehave

ROOT	SAMPLE WORD	*MEANING*
hyper- exces-sive, exces-sively	• hyperactive • hypercritical • hypersensitive	• overactive • over critical • over sensitive
inter- between, among	• international • interfaith • intertwine • intercellular • interject	• between nations • between faiths • to twine or twist together • between cells • to throw into
inter- between, among	• intervene • international	• come between • between nations
-ism **forms nouns** **and means** **"the act,** **state, or** **theory of"**	• criticism • optimism • capitalism	• act of being criti-cal • act of being op-timistic • practice of free enterprise
-ist **forms agent** **nouns from** **verbs ending** **in -ize or** **nouns ending** **in -ism and is** **used like -er**	• conformist • copyist • cyclist	• one who con-forms • one who copies • one who cycles

ROOT	SAMPLE WORD	*MEANING*
-ize **forms verbs** **from nouns** **and adjec-** **tives**	• formalize • jeopardize • legalize • modernize • emphasize • hospitalize • industrialize • computerize	• to make formal • to put in jeopardy • to make legal • to make modern • go give emphasis to • to put in hospital • to make industrial • to subject to computers
-ject-, to throw	• eject • inject • interject • project • reject • subject	• to throw out • to throw in • to throw in between, interrupt • to throw forward, make plans • to throw back, decline • to throw down, subdue
leg- law	• legislature • legitimate • legal	• law-making body • lawful • lawful
-logue, -log **speech, dis-** **course; to** **speak**	• monologue • dialogue • travelogue	• speech by one person • speech by two people • speech about travel

ROOT	SAMPLE WORD	*MEANING*
-logy dis- course, ex- pression; science, theory, study	• phraseology • biology • dermatology	• means of expres- sion • study of life • study of the skin
luc- light	• lucid • translucent • elucidate	• clear • permitting light through • enlighten, make clear
mal- bad	• malevolent • malediction • malefactor	• evil • curse, saying evil • evil-doer
man- hand	• manufacture • manuscript	• created, make by hand • writing by hand
-ment forms nouns from verbs	• entertain • entertainment • amaze • amazement	• amuse • amusement • astonish • astonishment
-meter, -metry measuring device; meas- ure	• geometry • kilometer • parameter • perimeter	• measurement (of land) • one thousand measures • constraint • boundary

ROOT	SAMPLE WORD	*MEANING*
micro- small	• microcosm • micronucleus • microscope	• A small, representative system • The smaller of two nuclei • device to magnify small objects
mono- one, single, alone	• monochrome • monosyllable • monoxide	• single color • single syllable • containing one oxygen atom
-morph- form	• amorphous • metamorphic • morphology	• lacking form • changed in structure • study of form and structure
neo- new, recent	• neonatal • neophyte •neoconservatism • neofascism • neodymium	• relating to newborn infants • novice • new conservative movement • new fascist movement • a rare earth metal: Nd

ROOT	SAMPLE WORD	*MEANING*
non- not	• nonessential • nonmetallic • nonresident • nonviolent • nonskid • nonstop	• not essential • not metallic • not a resident • lacking or opposed to violence • resistant to skidding • without stops
-oid **forms adjectives and nouns and means "like, resembling" or "shape, form"**	• humanoid • spheroid • trapezoid	• resembling a human • resembling a sphere • resembling a trapeze
pan- all	• panorama • panchromatic, • pandemic • pantheism	• extensive vista • sensitive to all colors • affecting many or all people • belief in god in everything
-path- **feeling, suffering**	• empathy • sympathy • apathy • apathetic • psychopathic	• compassion • consideration • indifference • indifferent • having an antisocial disorder

ROOT	SAMPLE WORD	*MEANING*
-pedo-, -ped- child, child- ren	• pediatrician • pedagogue	• doctor for child-ren • school teacher
-pel-, to drive	• compel • dispel • impel • repel	• force • disperse • hurl • drive back
-pend-, to hang	• append • depend • impend • pendant • pendulum	• attach • to rely upon • be about to hap-pen • item of hanging jewelry • a body that swings back and forth
-phile one that loves or has a strong affini-ty for; loving -philo-, -phil- having a strong affini-ty or love for	• audiophile • Francophile • philanthropy • philharmonic • philosophy	• one who loves sound • one who loves France • love of humanity • devoted to music • love of wisdom

ROOT	SAMPLE WORD	*MEANING*
-phobe, -phobia one that fears a specified thing; an intense fear of a specified thing	• agoraphobe • agoraphobia • xenophobe • xenophobia	• one who fears open spaces • fear of open spaces • one who fears foreigners • fear or loathing of foreigners
-phon- sound	• polyphonic • cacophony • phonetics	• having multiple musical sounds • combination of discordant sounds • study of the sounds of speech
-phone sound; device that receives or emits sound; speaker of a language	• homophone • geophone • telephone • Francophone	• words sharing the same sound • device for sensing earth sounds • device for hearing at a distance • one who sounds French
-port-, to carry	• comport • deport • export • import • report • support	• to carry oneself in a certain way • expel • send abroad • bring in • testimony • hold up

ROOT	SAMPLE WORD	*MEANING*
post- after	• postdate • postwar • postnasal • postnatal	• to date with a future date • after war • behind (after) the nose • occurring after birth
pre- before	• preconceive • preexist • premeditate • predispose • prepossess • prepay	• to opine before knowing • to exist before • to plan in advance • to incline previously • to preoccupy the mind • to pay in advance
re- again; back, backward	• rearrange • rebuild • recall • remake • rerun • rewrite	• to order again • to build again • call back to mind • to make again • to run again • to write over again
-scrib-, -script-, to write	• describe • prescription • subscribe • subscription • transcribe	• depict • recommendation • to sign at the bottom • underwrite • record

ROOT	SAMPLE WORD	*MEANING*
sub- under	• submarine • subsoil • subway • subhuman • substandard	• beneath the sea • soil lying below • underground train • beneath or less than human • below standard
thermo-, therm- heat	• thermal • thermometer • thermostat	• of or related to temperature • device for measuring temperature • device for controlling temperature
-tract-, to pull, drag, draw	• attract • contract • detract • extract • protract • retract • traction	• exert a pull on • bond • to draw or take away • to pull out • to draw forth over time • do draw back • grip, pulling stability
trans- across, beyond, through	• transatlantic • transpolar	• Atlantic crossing • crossing polar regions

ROOT	SAMPLE WORD	*MEANING*
-ty, -ity forms nouns from adjectives	• subtlety	• quality of being subtle
	• certainty	• quality of being certain
	• cruelty	• quality of being cruel
	• frailty	• quality of being frail
	• loyalty	• quality of being loyal
	• royalty	• quality of being royal
	• eccentricity	• quality of being eccentric
	• electricity	• that which is electric
	• peculiarity	• quality of being peculiar
	• similarity	• quality of being similar
	• technicality	• technical detail
-vert-, to turn	• convert	• alter
	• divert	• redirect
	• invert	• reverse
	• revert	• turn back
vid, vis- to see	• vision	• sight
	• evidence	• items seen

ROOT	SAMPLE WORD	*MEANING*
voc- to call	• avocation • provocation • invocation	• calling, minor occupation • calling or rousing to anger • calling in prayer

Appendix D

Online Resources

A complete collection of resources mentioned in these pages together with additional material is available at:
http:// abacus-es.com/cpep/resources.html

Index

Made in the USA
Charleston, SC
29 September 2011